[LEE BROWN]

**FOREWORDS BY LEANOR ORTEGA TILL OF FIVE IRON FRENZY
AND SETH HECOX OF BECOMING THE ARCHETYPE**

[WHO IS THIS GOD PERSON, *ANYWAY?*]

"It is also the story of a book, a book called *The Hitchhiker's Guide to the Galaxy* - not an Earth book, never published on Earth… nevertheless, a wholly remarkable book. In fact, it was probably the most remarkable book ever to come out of the great publishing corporations of Ursa Minor - which no earther had ever heard either.

Not only is it a wholly remarkable book, it is also a highly successful one - more popular than *The Celestial Home Care Omnibus*, better selling than *Fifty-three More Things to Do in Zero Gravity*, and more controversial than Oolon Coluphid's trilogy of philosophical blockbusters, *Where God Went Wrong, Some More of God's Greatest Mistakes,* and *Who is This God Person, Anyway?"*

- Douglas Adams, *The Hitchhiker's Guide to the Galaxy*

[*Acknowledgements*]

"Atheism is hardly worse than building life around a wrong concept of God. Lee Brown rightly believes that the closer we come to Jesus the more we will understand properly. He digs deep, comes close, shows the way, respects Biblical revelation, samples the best Christian thinkers, and radiates real life with a flare for clear and practical writing. I commend these pages to all searchers after the biggest truth of all—the only God who really is, and who is so worth knowing!"

BARRY L. CALLEN, Author of the bestselling books *God as Loving Grace, God in the Shadows, and Discerning the Divine*

"Do you ask questions? Do you wish someone took the real questions seriously? Wouldn't it be great if there was a single place where someone would take the most important questions seriously? That's what Lee Brown has done in his new book. Read it. Savor it. Question it. Think."

STEVE RENNICK, Executive Director, Advance Colorado

"Extremely well-written and engaging. The questions addressed and the process the reader will go on is fresh, insightful, and compelling. A book for anyone willing to grapple with important questions about God, life, and the core message of the Gospel."

ROD STAFFORD, Lead Pastor, Fairfax Community Church and author of *Free to Lead*

"Engaging and fun, this book takes the reader on a personal journey of exploration in the never-ending quest to understand who God really is. The author uses his own life experiences to raise issues of eternal import, and challenges the reader to think deeply about them. I have long been convinced that most - if not all - of our psychological problems are a result of what I call 'bad theology.' If there's any truth to that, Lee Brown will help individuals and small groups confront some bad theology, judge it appropriately, and construct some 'good theology.' I recommend this book to your consideration."

JOHN H. AUKERMAN, Professor Emeritus, Anderson University

"Life can be a complicated business. The challenges, opportunities, and passions that dare us day-by-day can keep us from taking a deep breath and wrestling with the irreducible prime. How did I get here, anyway? What am I doing here? Is there something, some One, before me and after me, outside of time, but active in my world? Is there a God? And, if so, so what? The 'if' and 'so what' hold the keys to everything else. Dive into Brown's thoughtful (and so fun to read) quest. You'll be better for it. And, so will your view of the world."

JIM LYON, General Director of Church of God Ministries, Author of *Jesus B.*, and anchor of *Viewpoint*

"I know Lee Brown as a student and colleague in ministry. He distinguished himself as a student and has taken that same approach to ministry. Lee has written a book that is both a labor of love for others to know the fullness of following Jesus, as well as the result of his deep love in following Jesus for himself. I encourage you to read and apply what you find in these pages, you will be better for it."

CLIFF SANDERS, Chair of Biblical Studies, Mid-America Christian University, and author of *The Optimism of Grace,* and *Making Sense Out of Spirituality* *Acknowledgement originally published in Lee's prior book *Here's How: An Introduction to Practical Discipleship.*

"Lee is a young, intelligent, and enthusiastic leader. His passion for spiritual growth is evident in his writing. He is a key leader in the church of the future."

MARTY GRUBBS, Lead Pastor, Crossings Community Church and Author of *Restored: Getting Back to Who You We're Meant To Be.* *Acknowledgement originally published in Lee's prior book *Here's How: An Introduction to Practical Discipleship.*

Who Is This God Person, Anyway?
© 2019 by Lee Brown

Who Is This God Person, Anyway? By Lee Brown
Published by Sloan's Lake Church // Next Step Resources
2796 Utica St, Denver CO 80212
www.sloanslake.church

Graphics design by Kyle Younkman. kyounkman@gmail.com

Page Layout by Lee Brown.

Unless otherwise indicated, Scripture quotations are from the Christian Standard Bible® (CSB). Scripture quotations marked CSB have been taken from the Christian Standard Bible®, Copyright © 2017 by Holman Bible Publishers. Used by permission. Christian Standard Bible® and CSB® are federally registered trademarks of Holman Bible Publishers.

Although men and woman whose stories are told in this book are real, names may have been changed to protect their privacy.

While the author has made every effort to provide accurate Internet addresses at the time of publication, neither the publisher nor the author assumes any responsibility for errors or changes that occur after publication.

Printed in the United States of America.

[For Renae, Logan, and Jazzy.]

I'm so glad God made our adventures to be together.

May you become more like Jesus every day.

[*Table of Contents*]

[*FOREWORD*]
BY SETH HECOX

Asking the questions that Douglas Adams asked is never a bad idea. Lee Brown does just that, and asks the right question: who, exactly, is this God we all talk about?

The notion of God, or of Truth, for that matter, is a slippery subject. We humans crave absolutes. We want certainty. We demand hard and fast answers. But, if there's one thing we can learn from people's experiences with God, it's that God is quite difficult to pin down.

The Hebrew Bible depicts God telling humans, "my thoughts are not your thoughts, nor are your ways my ways" (Isaiah 55:8). Later, in the earliest writings of the Apostle Paul, he asks, "Who has known the mind of the Lord?" (Romans 11:34 and 1 Corinthians 2:16).

In our search for Truth and in our thoughts about God, it serves us best to hold things lightly. This is why I'm so thrilled that the title of this book is a question. It sets the tone for much of its content: questions and exploring. So often, Jesus taught through questions, rather than answer-giving. He seemed most pleased when His disciples asked the right questions, even when He did not give them the answer in a straight-forward manner (or at all).

As a seminary student at George Fox Theological Seminary, I was astounded, and sometimes overwhelmed, at the sheer multitude of perspectives about God that existed even within the broader Christian faith. Being exposed to those perspectives and considering them honestly helps keep our faith nimble, flexible, and alive. Without that exposure, our faith quickly becomes brittle and dead, and the results can be devastating.

Although I tend not to give definite answers to members of my congregation about such unknowable topics (God, the afterlife, the "anti-vax" movement, etc.), I love exploring the most far-ranging and sometimes previously un-thought-of questions with them.

Is God good?

Could God be bad?

What does God look like as a mother?

Is God omnipotent, or does God perhaps contain (or use) no power?

When we grapple with these questions, we each grow, so long as we don't immediately high-tail it back to the safety of our previous certainties. God may be mostly unknowable, but it seems to me that God is not the Author of fear. Fear is the only thing that might hold you back as you venture into the dark woods of unknowing.

The truth is slippery, yes. But as Fox Mulder might say, "The Truth is out there," even if we can't quite grasp it. Still, there's no harm in exploring.

Reverend Seth Hecox
Pastor of Grace Lutheran Church (Wilmington, IL)
Founding member of Becoming the Archetype

[*FOREWORD*]
BY LEANOR ORTEGA TILL

Let me begin by saying that I don't wholly enjoy reading theology books. That being confessed, I have to say that Lee Brown's *Who Is This God Person, Anyway?* is much more than a theology book. You can tell right off the bat, because, well, this book is very *readable*.

I would go so far as to say it is delightfully entertaining, which is why I am hoping you take the time to sit with this book and truly read it. Because Lee draws from a wide birth of quotes, stories, and sci-fi metaphors, this book reads like a journal of a typical American dude that has an interesting, insatiable quest for a life with more meaning, a quest to meet up with the sacred.

Who doesn't want that?

It goes without saying that to answer the question of Who God is might be one of the most daunting feats one can hope to conquer! With that in mind, Lee does not attempt to merely quote the Bible, rather, he finds God and learns about the Person of God as lived in his own day to day life.

Life for Lee was rural, American, typical in some ways of modern culture, but he also has had his share of struggles. It is those struggles that inform his view of God; as they do for us all. For instance, how does a man raised without a father figure wrestle with the image of God as Father?

To his credit, Lee goes deep when sharing about such a dilemma. From his boldness in sharing *Mere Christianity* with a non-believing academic, to more matters of the heart when it comes to raising his adopted daughter, Jazzy, Lee appeals to the reader's heart and spirit, as well as their mind.

So often we walk alongside others wondering how they really hear God. Do they really hear God? How can they believe that there is an all-knowing God that loves them and why would this God love them if He really knew how broken they were?

It's not often that general society gets a peek into another's spiritual story with its brokenness, questions, successes, and even, at times, arrogance. For that reason, I appreciate Lee's attempt at making his own story and intimate relationship with "This God Person" known.

Leanor Ortega Till
Saxophonist for Five Iron Frenzy
Pastoral Staff at Sloan's Lake Church (Denver, CO)

[ONE]

THE ANSWER TO LIFE, THE UNIVERSE, AND EVERYTHING

Also Known As "The Intro"

It does not pain me in the slightest to say that this book is wholly incomplete. Truly, the subject matter itself could never be complete. Trying to say "this book contains everything there is to know about God," is like a soda can reveling in the fact that it has swallowed the ocean, when, in reality, it is only full in itself.

That soda can may be full, but the oceans rage on past the horizon. This is a little bit of what one faces when writing a finite book on the subject of the infinite. To say that this book is a complete account of God would be utterly laughable.

In his bestselling sci-fi classic *The Hitchhiker's Guide to the Galaxy*, author Douglas Adams imagines such an infinite book. This book contains all of the greatest thinking in the history of the universe, and yet, *The Hitchhiker's Guide to the Galaxy* - the book that we read, not the book the characters in the book read from - is not really about a book at all. It is the pursuit of a question.

In the story, a group of "hyper-intelligent pan-dimensional beings" get so fed up with the constant bickering over the meaning of life that they create the most astounding computer ever imagined - up to the 1980's, at least. This computer is tasked with finding **THE** answer. **THE** answer to life, the universe, and everything. This computer, which is the size of a football stadium in the film version, tells its masters that it will need seven-and-a-half million years to complete its calculations.

A brief seven-and-a-half million years later, many civilizations from across the universe enthusiastically come to hear its answer. Deep Thought - that's the computer's name - warns its masters that they are not going to like the result and then calmly spits out the answer to life, the universe, and everything.

"It's 42," by the way. "No, really, it is 42," Deep Thought assures before making the most astute observation a near omniscient artificial being could make. "It would have been better to know the question."

Here we discover the true purpose of this book; the question. **THE** question behind the meaning of life, the universe, and everything. But, if a pan-dimensional supercomputer imagined up in the height of human technology, the 1980's, cannot decipher **THE** question, how can any human being hope to do so?

Perhaps we yet have an advantage over even this most baffling computer. As another British author, J. B. Philips, has said, "If it is true that there is Someone in charge of the whole mystery of life and death, we can hardly expect to escape a sense of futility and frustration until we begin to see what He is like and what His purposes are[1]." And so the great struggle begins.

To seek God is to seek the infinite, to peer into the depths of time and creation itself. As humans, we are finite objects who could never get our wrists around something so beyond us and unknowable. Pastor Chris Hodges notes, "If God always has to fit everything into our understanding, if He always has to fit into our limited human minds, then He will always be less. He will be a very small god whom we can handle, a very safe god who never disrupts our lives[2]."

Yet, to say that we cannot know God, at least in so far as He has revealed Himself to mankind, is equally as ignorant. History reveals a God who desires to be known. God Himself reveals to us sweet vapors of Who He is.

Certainly, we cannot know ALL of God anymore than a soda can can swallow the ocean or the 1980's could actually produce an all-knowing computer, but, God has revealed Himself to us in many ways so that we can know... *some* of Him. He has revealed Himself through what theologians call "general revelation." That is to say, things like nature and wisdom - the way things are designed to work.

He has also given us some very specific revelation of His nature and character, most importantly, through the Bible and the historic life, nature, and character of Jesus the Christ. So, while we may never have a full grasp on God - after all the Biblical book of Revelation pictures angels covered with eyes who circle the throne of God who <u>never</u> stop seeing new and amazing things about Him - what He has shown us of Himself is more than we need to keep us in awe for all of eternity.

While there is a great deal that can be learned of God through nature, the movement of the planets, and the way life has been designed to work, it is through the specific revelation of the Bible and Jesus the Christ that our quest will begin.

Why through the Bible? The Bible is a source worth considering for even the most hardened skeptic. There has never been a more tested, doubted, mocked, or more proven book in all of history. Some of the greatest minds ever to have lived - not to mention supercomputers - have attempted to disprove the Bible, yet, they are gone and it remains... unscathed.

The Bible has long sat as history's true number one bestselling book. However, it is not like other books. In fact, it is not really a book at all. It is a library of books and letters, comprised of 66 writings by over 40 different authors and was written over a span in excess of 1,500 years! Yet, in spite of the fact that you can't say something in a room of 15 people and go 15 minutes without your message being distorted, this "book" has no major inconsistency in the message of the text.

Simply put, there has never been another book like this in history. That alone makes it worth considering. This is doubly so, then, when we find that this library of books has a uniform voice and message that all points back to the Creator of the universe, unveiling glimmers of His nature and character. The entire witness of every page points the reader back to Jesus, to Whom this book will also turn.

While we may have only a glimmer of a whisper of a shadow of any understanding about God at all, what He has revealed to us gives us what we need to make some statements about who God is... and who God certainly is not.

Incidentally, if you are one who doubts the truth of what many call Scripture, I would advise that you commit every waking hour of your life to disproving it, for the good of everyone. If it is false in any way, we should all know about it. But, if, like the many thousands of genius-level skeptics who have come and gone, you cannot disprove it, you will have accomplished something great for your own journey that cannot be taken away from you.

This is the aim of the book you are holding. It is the pursuit of a question. **THE** question that leads to the meaning of life, the universe, and everything. While it is the best I have been able to come up with in my limited lifespan, it is far from complete. It is much more like a soda can, swimming in an infinite ocean, letting in as much water as it is able to hold, all the while itself being suspended by, shrouded around, and floating in that very same ocean.

[*TWO*]

THE FOUNDATION OF THE UNIVERSE

Don't Panic.

> "What comes to mind when we think of God
> is the most important thing about us."
> **A. W. Tozer, *The Knowledge of the Holy***

I distinctly remember which day in history it was because of how it intersected with one of my own major life events. It was my wife and I's fifth wedding anniversary. For five years we had looked forward to this day and dreamed of how we might go to Disneyland or return to the tropical island where we had spent our honeymoon.

Instead, we found ourselves mobilizing rescue crews to go back into the wreckage. It wasn't until Facebook chimed my phone that either of us even realized what day it was. It had been a whirlwind - no pun intended - of a season for us. I'd like to point out for the record that it was I who "remembered" our anniversary first; a fact that mattered so little that day.

It was a Tuesday when it happened. Having lived in Moore, Oklahoma for some time, I was not unfamiliar with tornado season. When I had first moved there, I had been rather nervous about this sort of weather. That first time the sirens went off, something in me panicked. I was aghast to see my Okie-native roommate so brazenly calm.

"Shouldn't we go to a shelter or something?" I asked with a noticeable panic in my voice.

My roommate paused his video game. He casually walked over to our dorm-room door. As he opened it, I could see that the air all around us had turned a sickening shade of yellow. This made me gulp even harder as I waited for him to rush us to safety.

After a moment of staring out into the skies, as I imagine a weathered sea captain on rocky waters would do, he stared calmly into the distance and proclaimed, "Eh. It's not coming this way," and immediately returned to his video game.

It mattered if he was right.

While Kyle's nonchalant attitude about one of nature's greatest death machines shocked me at the time, over the years I also grew so used to them that a healthy fear had all but left me. My roommate Shawn and I even foolishly chased a tornado one time… for funzies. Perhaps that was why, some years later, my pastor and I were joking around and trying to get our computer network back up and running as the 4Warn storm team began their desperate pleas.

These seasoned storm trackers had been blindsided by how fast a section of air that looked to be calming down had suddenly become a history-shattering F-5 tornado. This wasn't any average Oklahoma tornado. This one was a big one. This tornado, in fact, would end up growing to around a mile and a half wide, and it would stay on the ground for just over 17 straight miles.

My wife called me with an unusual sense of panic in her voice. Far from being afraid of the annual storms that rip through her home state, she would watch the tornado coverage with a hint of masochistic glee in her eyes. Having grown up in Oklahoma, she had always dreamed of becoming a storm chaser, herself.

This time, however, she was afraid. She asked me to get home as fast as possible. I could tell by the tone of her voice that she was frighteningly serious. Not much more than fifteen minutes later, we were in a neighbor's storm shelter desperately trying to hear a small radio as hail pummeled the thick metal door and my 14 month-old son played obliviously on the cold floor. A flickering light in the tiny concrete room combined with the sound of hurricane force winds and golfball sized hail only added to the experience that around a dozen people crammed into a 5 x 5 room were all going through together.

Our crackling storm-radio carried the voice of Mike Morgan, the trusted local weatherman, who was repeatedly saying "If you are above ground, you are going to die." Time passes very slowly in moments like that. Your mind tends to wander. We began to imagine what the world above us might look like. We began to ask ourselves if our house would still be standing... If our church would be okay... if our friends were alive... whether we had properly said our goodbyes to family.

Nothing could prepare us, either, for what we would see when we safely stepped out of that storm shelter. Miles upon miles of property had been destroyed. Homes had been lost. Lives had ended. Our city suddenly looked like one of those scenes Hollywood spends millions of dollars making from the comfort of their computers, except the real-life version was much harder to stomach.

We were lucky enough to have sustained no damage to our home. The church was untouched. But thousands were not as lucky as we were. As we got back into our house, we found that we were without power. We knew this would likely not be of high priority over the next few days. We didn't know what else to do. Phone lines were down. All of the networks were jammed. So, we decided to drive around.

As we drove closer to the tornado's path, we saw some crazy things - the kind you hear about and immediately imagine are just made up to make someone's story sound more interesting, like where a splinter of wood is found having impaled itself clean through a slab of concrete, or a telephone pole was shattered only at the base, so that the cables lifted it up to display the form of a cross as a sign of hope to a devastated community. I believe I still have pictures of both.

The billboard we had often passed by on the highway had also inconveniently relocated itself into the living room of the house next to some of our best friends. This significantly lessened the impact of those $19.99 oil changes it was advertising. Many of the houses between theirs and ours had also relocated themselves elsewhere against their will.

Somehow, we ended up in the parking lot of our local Crest grocery store. There we met a nice elderly couple who had just hours ago lost everything they ever owned, except their lives. They were not alone. In the days that would follow, we would encounter many people, even some in our own church, who lost their homes and all of their earthly possessions.

It is in times like this when you realize that those material things aren't really as important as you thought they were. Tv's, cars, homes, billboards promoting $19.99 oil changes, even family pictures matter little, so long as your loved ones are okay. So long as you are together.

My wife, son, and I ended up sleeping for a few days in my office at the church while we waited for our power to come back on at our home. There, we watched in horror as 24 lives were reported to be lost, several of them children in one of the two elementary schools that once stood in the path of this monster.

In the morning, we started cleaning up around the church. Every inch of our property, though untouched by the violence, was covered in insulation, wood splinters, and pictures, of all things. It is hard to imagine a scene like that if you've never experienced it first-hand.

It was in this early morning light that we began to see the first glimpse of God's grace. As I began making a small dent in a tremendous mess, I somehow came across a mangled picture of the couple we had met at the grocery store just the day before.

Out of all the houses that were destroyed…

For all the millions of dollars of property that was rearranged inconveniently all over the city…

I just happened to come across a personal picture of a couple we had never met prior to the day of the tornado. The odds that I would find that particular picture of that particular couple were astronomically small. Yet, there it was.

Days later, another wave of tornadoes unexpectedly struck the city, just barely north of where the first round had hit. Some of the most seasoned storm chasers in the industry lost their lives in that horrific event. Flash flooding also became a serious issue.

In one of nature's most horrifying practical jokes, the Oklahoma red clay often expands and contracts with the weather, sometimes causing underground shelters to surface in severe flooding. This is not the best thing to have happen, as tornadoes just love to rip everything off of the ground. It was a rather unfortunate combination.

As Emily Sutton would put it on the news that day, "It is still May in Oklahoma, unfortunately."

Sometime after the President made his visit and home-town boy, Toby Keith, had come to view the devastation, I found myself once again out in the field. While I had witnessed Joplin several weeks after their most devastating storm, nothing could prepare me for what I would see in the days immediately following that second round of storm systems.

Trees were mangled and twisted in ways that I couldn't understand. Cars were sitting part-way through the walls of houses. Others were flattened as if they had been compacted in a vice. Where houses still partially stood, orange spray paint marked them to let people know that emergency crews had cleared the home, checking for anyone trapped in the rubble.

However, it was where the houses no longer stood that made the greatest impression on me. That was a scene I will never forget. Where once stood a sea of houses, swing sets, cars, and a bustling economy that was still rebounding from the 2008 recession, now, as far as my eyes could see, there was nothing but a series of foundations and debris.

The foundations in particular caught my eye. Everything else was wiped away... but the foundations still stood. This image imprinted itself into my mind, and it is most fitting to the conversation I hope to have through the course of this book. You see, we build our lives on a lot of things. Some of us build our lives on our jobs. Some on our families. Some build their lives on their nationality. Some on their personal accomplishments.

No matter what we use as the brick and mortar to build our lives, it cannot compare to the importance of the foundation upon which we construct them. Each of us will go through trials, battles, and perhaps even a few natural disasters. It is in those moments where the mettle of our lives will be tested. If the foundation upon which we have built our lives is sturdy, we can withstand the storms. However, if our foundation is weak, cracked, or crumbling, the storms of life will devastate us until we have nothing left.

Shortly after these storms hit where I then lived (I have since moved to where tornadoes and allergies are less likely to end my existence on this earth), a religious group who became infamous for their creative use of colorful signs and protests began speaking out against our city, proclaiming that these twin storms were God's judgement for its rampant immorality.

It matters if they were right.

What we believe about God is the foundation of our lives. Even if you say that you don't believe in any god, each of us has a throne in our lives from which all other decisions are made. That idea, thing, or person that you place in the ruling seat of your life still remains. Each of us have something that works as the deepest level of life's meta-narrative. Either we bow to a god or we place another object, most often ourselves, as the ultimate decider of reality, becoming our own self-god.

In his letter to the Corinthians, a formerly uptight and highly religious leader named Paul shares with a young church all they need to know about life. "According to God's grace that was given to me, I have laid a foundation as a skilled master builder, and another builds on it. But each one is to be careful how he builds on it. For no one can lay any other foundation than what as been laid down. That foundation is Jesus Christ" (1 Corinthians 3:10-11 CSB).

Jesus must be our foundation. He is what we build the rest of life and our perception of reality upon. He is the only thing that will remain when everything else falls apart. He is what is revealed more clearly when the storms of life hit. Because of that, our relationship with God is the single most important aspect of life to consider.

What we believe about the nature and character of God is the firm foundation upon which life, the universe, and everything is built. While we rarely give much thought to our foundations, literally everything else we believe is built upon them. This foundation is, therefore, the most important piece of our brain or spirit, science or theology, that we could ever explore.

This is the lens through which we see all of life. Like the glasses that I didn't know I needed until years ago, everything we see is shaped by Who we say God is. If our glasses are dirty, dark, smudged, or out of focus the world we see around us will be, as well.

If our foundation is cracked, the walls that we build upon it will crack and shift. If our foundation is crumbled, we will not withstand life's storms. That is why all of life's other questions come back to this one question… this core foundational question about life, the universe, and everything.

THE question:

Who Is This God Person, Anyway?

[For Personal Growth]

Take a moment and make a list of everything you believe about God. Leave no stone unturned. Once you have written down what you believe about God, go back through this list and begin processing where it is you got these beliefs.

If possible, compare this list with what you currently know about your Bible.

[With A Group]

Go around the group and share what you personally believe about God (who God is, God's nature and character), and where you got that idea from.

Have someone read Psalm 9:10. In Biblical times, the word "name" wasn't just what someone called you by, but also signified a person's expected character.

Knowing this, what does it mean that if we know God's "name" (nature and character) we will trust in Him?

What would need to change in your understanding of God for you to trust Him?

If there is time, share and discuss anything else from this chapter that challenged you.

Before you close in prayer, have each person share with the group what measurable and practical way you are going to respond to God this week.

[My Next Step]

[THREE]

THE CRACK IN THE UNIVERSE
As Seen From the Bedroom Wall of One Amelia Pond.

> "If you have an incorrect view of God, the more religious you are, the worse it is. It would be better for you to be an atheist."
> **William Temple**

As we were preparing to sell our house in Oklahoma, we received some potentially terrible news. We needed a full inspection done on the foundation of our home. Our realtor took us around to the side of our starter house and pointed her well-manicured finger to where she wanted our eyes to travel.

It was obvious what she was seeing. Long cracks ran along the side of our house in an area we rarely saw due to some concealing shrubbery. This explained why the bedroom doors didn't quite close right, and why thin lines were beginning to show along our bedroom walls.

This revelation brought a substantial amount of dread upon us. Fixing a foundation is not cheap, nor is it easy. Yet, if we hoped to ever sell our house, this inspection must be done. Few buyers would take on a house with a bad foundation. It is a kiss of death.

If the foundation is bad, everything that is built on top of it will eventually begin to reveal problems that have been hiding for years, perhaps even decades. The integrity of the foundation matters immensely, and it was clear that our foundation was pulling itself apart. Were this left unchecked, our house's problems would only intensify.

Everything in a house depends on its firm foundation. No matter how pretty the home might be that sits upon it, a house with a bad foundation is headed for problems and potentially expensive repairs. Ask any realtor. They will tell you the same.

This is why it matters whether the sign-bearing people who plagued Oklahoma after the tornadoes were right. You see, they were simply building upon their foundation. Their actions flowed out of what they believed about God. It caused them to pronounce judgement and proclaim loudly exactly what God hated about us and our city.

Best-selling suspense author Ted Dekker has noted that, "what you do will flow from what you believe[3]." The most basic foundational element of our lives is what we believe about God. This is the first building block of all reality. This is the foundation upon which <u>everything</u> else is built. It shapes every choice we make, every single day. Our view of God is the lens through which we see all of the rest of life. It impacts everything we do.

It's not just the sign-waivers who potentially have cracks in their foundation, however. We are quick to point fingers at others, yet I would argue that each of us should examine our own foundation. We often don't realize the cracks are there until the storms of life come. We become all too comfortable with the cracks in the wall in our own houses. We notice them less with each passing day. Yet, we are often quickly able to see the cracks in the walls of other peoples' homes. We would do ourselves a favor to begin by first inspecting our own house.

One morning while I was a youth pastor in Oklahoma, I found that I had a voicemail message from the wee hours of the night that I had slept through. Once I listened to the voicemail, I was off to the hospital as quickly as I could legally get there.

I arrived in the ER to see one of my youth sitting on a hospital bench, pale. The night before she had broken up with her boyfriend. This now-ex had... not taken the break up well. At first, he had simply snuck out and gotten drunk with his friends. Drunkenness, however, soon turned to anger. He returned in the middle of the night and began kicking the house near his ex-girlfriend's bedroom. Soon, he began to knock on her windows. Then, he began pounding them with his fists.

Before long, in his inebriated state, he put his arm through her window. I imagine this scene resembled something from a horror movie as his bloody arm reached through this girl's bedroom window. It was about to get much worse. Upon pulling his arm back through the broken glass, he shredded every major artery and vessel. Bleeding out, he crawled back home to his mother, who lived across the street. She frantically called 9-1-1 and sat on his arm to try and stop the bleeding until help could arrive.

By the time I has shown up that next day, the ex-boyfriend had been in surgery for many hours. Gallons of blood had been pumped through him. Doctors were frantically doing everything they could to save this young man's life.

Shortly after I arrived, the doctors asked the mother and family to come into a private room. As the closest available pastor, I was asked to come along, as well. The air in the room was thick with nervous sweat and tears. The doctor sat in silence much longer than any of us were comfortable with.

Finally, after swallowing noticeably, he began to share with this fearful mother the slim odds that her son would live through the next hour. Tears came. Violent tears. Understandable violent tears. For a long time, no one said anything. The doctor sat in silence. The family stared at the floor.

The next words spoken came from his mother. I looked up at her. She was staring a hole through me. My eyes got wide. Silence filled the room. Then she spoke.

"He did it again. That piece of ****. He did it again."

I didn't know what to do or say. I had graduated from Bible college, but somehow my professors neglected to train me for this exact moment. I'm not sure they could have.

"Why does He keep taking my children from me? Why does YOUR GOD keep taking my children from me?"

She kept staring at me. I think she wanted an answer. I would later find out that this woman's daughter had been killed by a car years before. I didn't know what to say, yet something arose from somewhere deep inside... nearer to my foundation.

I don't remember what I said... but, I believe it was a musing on how God doesn't cause the bad that comes into our lives, but that He is there with us in those moments... and His heart was breaking for His child, too. I suggested that He had likely reached out as the boys were grabbing beers... that He had pleaded with the teen not to go over to her house, but to cool off and go to bed.

It matters if I was right.

A lot was at stake in that moment. A lot was at stake when her son passed away on the operating table. A lot was at stake as I stood in front of a room filled with that boy's family and hundreds of classmates and delivered his eulogy.

Was God the sort of God who takes the lives of teenage boys who drunkenly terrorize their ex-girlfriends? Or had this teen's choices had life-ending consequences? Had God tried to reach out to this young man to get him to choose another course of action that night?

It matters what sort of God, God is. Especially to broken mothers. Especially when you're trying to pick up the pieces of a broken life. Especially to frightened young pastors. Especially when things get ugly real. It matters Who God really and truly is.

Unfortunately, it is often not until everything falls apart that we truly examine our foundation. When things are "normal" or "good" we don't give much thought to Who God is. It isn't until the cracks in the wall become hard to ignore before we are finally willing to pay for an inspection. After all, foundations are difficult to repair, and the process is more costly than we're comfortable paying.

I would argue that a great majority of us have cracks in our foundation. Even those who have followed God for many years, if they have not more carefully examined what they believe, are at risk for serious cracks. This should be alarming to us. It should cause us to call for an inspection, because whatever the inspection costs... the cost of ignoring the cracks is so much greater in the long run.

Why Consider What We Believe About God?

What if what we believe about God is wrong? Everything that is built upon a bad foundation is at risk of crumbling. Dr. Cliff Sanders, whose teachings led to the creation of this work, has stated, "If there is a God, it should be your life's business to know Him correctly for Who He is and what He respects. The foundation for Christian living is knowing the kind of God that God really is." Steven Furtick has added, "every disfunction begins with a distortion about who God is. That's why, in addition to knowing who He is, it's important to understand who He isn't[4]."

Think of it in these terms. Imagine life as a trip that you are taking with the aid of a GPS. Before you leave home, you plug directions into the GPS, which in turn tells you how to get where you are going. Now, imagine that you plug in the wrong destination. The GPS will kindly tell you where to make each turn, but it will never get you where you intended to go.

Should you discover that you are aiming at the wrong destination, you will not get where you intended to go any faster by slamming on the gas. You will not get to where you intended to go at all by making "progress" according to that GPS's guidance.

Progress is only possible by reestablishing the proper destination. This may even mean going back to where you started your journey. It may feel like you're wasting a lot of time, but continuing on the path you were on before will never get you there. You have to reroute to the proper destination if you are going to succeed at all.

Having an incorrect view of God is like being on a journey towards the wrong destination. The worst possible thing you can do if you're on the wrong path is to go further. The worst thing you can do if you have an improper view of God is to become further devoted to this caricature or image. Progress is actually found in going back to where you began and starting again.

Christianity is a relationship with God. The basis for trust in any relationship is found in getting to know the other person for who they really are. Trust and commitment come from a deepening knowledge of one another. We cannot get to know God more deeply if we are throwing ourselves at caricatures and half-truths that sit in His rightful place. That would be like trying to have a deepening relationship with a picture a person posted on their social account in place of the real, flesh and blood being.

How Did We Get Our Distorted Views of God?

There are two primary places that we, as human beings, develop distorted views of God. The first is found in significant relationships early in life. Social scientists say that much of how we see the world is shaped very early on by our relationship with our parents, or lack thereof.

To this end, your view of God is often a direct result of your early relationship with your father. Why your father and not your mother? Certainly both play a role in how you see God. In fact, in a healthy development, you are shown two different sides of the nature and beauty of God from each of your parents. However, we tend to see God firstly through the lens of our earthly father.

The basic structure of your personality is said to be formed around the age of five. So, your early relationship with your parents is crucial in your development. If your father, in particular, was distant as a young child, you'll find that God, no matter how devoted to Him you are, often seems very distant, as well. If your parents were cruel and punished you for every little transgression, no matter the size, you'll find that you see God as always out to catch and punish you.

Pastor, author, and podcaster Carey Nieuwhof has noted that this current generation is the most fatherless generation in known history who did not lose their father to war[5]. This alone tells me that whoever finds themselves reading this book is seriously at risk for a cracked foundation. As unfortunate or fortunate as you may have been in your early relationship with your parents, that relationship has left ripples that daily affect the way you view God and interact with Him.

The second way that we have developed a cracked foundation or distorted our view of God is through uncritically reflecting on life. Critical thinking is not taught to growing minds any longer. As a result of this, so much of what happens to us in our life goes uncritically examined and improperly processed.

Lucas Miles has noted that, "as the events of our lives unfold, our interpretation of those happenings has caused us to invent a god who is the author of the beliefs we now have of ourselves[6]." In other words, when we can't make sense of things or feel like we are out of options, we default to "it must have been God." This can lead to severely damaging repercussions.

After that lovely mother sat through my eulogy about her son, many people came up to her to console her. Doubtless, at least one or two of them uttered a phrase similar to "we just don't understand God's will sometimes. He must have just needed one more angel up there in heaven."

Dave Dooley, the pastor whom I served under at the time, was told this same rhetoric on the day of his father's funeral. Dave's father, a coal miner, had been tragically killed when Dave was still very young. Pastor Dooley has stated just how damaging those words were to him. "What kind of a God," he reasoned, "would take the father of a young boy away from him?" Sure, "God may have needed him," he recounts, "but don't you think I needed him more?"

When we attribute things to God's will that weren't His will, we risk creating a monster who takes our family members from us because either He is mad at them, or is lacking something that He can only gain by taking them away from us. In either case, this God is too small to be God of all.

We often give too much emphasis to "God's will." Biblically, there are at least three "wills" in the universe. God's will is only one of them. Truly, it is the greatest will of all, but God has also self-limited His power by giving His creation the ability to choose other than His will. Thus, there is also our own free will, which God has sovereignly allowed to overcome even His will for us. There is also the will of the original fallen angel and his regime of devils who come to steal, kill, and destroy (see John 10:10).

Pastor Lucas Miles has noted that, "Everything does happen for a reason, but that doesn't mean God is behind each and every reason. To see all our situations as 'God's plan' not only strips people of their responsibility to choose, but it also villainizes God and blames Him for the circumstances we experience in the world... In fact, much of the pain of this life has human choice, not God, at its epicenter[7]."

God designed life to be a system where the will of man can thwart the will of God. Look at the Parable of the Sower and the Seed for an example of this. Or, look to that heartbroken teenage boy. Was it God's will for him to get drunk and accidentally end his life that fateful night? Or did he choose something other than God's best for him and end up paying tragic consequences?

This question matters. How we answer it matters immensely.

When significant events happen in our life that we cannot explain, we simply chalk it up to God's will as a way of dealing with things. The irony in this is that we are really just postponing dealing with the issue and we end up making God our mental, emotional, or spiritual scapegoat, instead. Dr. Cliff Sanders has said of this, "Many people begin to ascribe to God all of the terrible things that have happened in their lives... if we cannot explain it, we assume God did it[8]."

In doing this, we attribute events and actions to the character of God that are really not His doing at all, or, worse, that contradict His character outright. The character of God is too important to allow this to happen. Scripture spends too much time explaining the character of God for us to allow uncritical reflection to crack our foundation.

So, how do we know if we have a distorted view of God? Our first thought might be to track down all of the misconceptions we have and eliminate them. But, how would we know what is a misconception if we don't first discover who God really is?

Have you ever come across a counterfeit bill in your life? Some counterfeits are easy to spot. They look like someone printed them at home using a low-res photo they found on Google Images. Others are much more difficult to discern.

Do you know how the government trains agents to discover counterfeits? They must spend hours every day looking into every new way that thieves have come up with to fake money, right?

Actually, no. They don't spend much time studying the fakes at all. Instead, they study the real thing. The more intimately familiar an agent is with real money, the easier it will be to spot a distortion. Spotting any sort of distortion gives away the counterfeit, even the most convincing one.

This is why we must dig into the Bible and examine the revelation of Jesus the Christ wherever possible. While it would be tempting to examine every passing trend that distorts Who God is (new ones are coming at us all the time), the best way to know if something is a fake or distortion, is to more intimately know the real deal. While I will tackle a selection of the most rampant distortions of the nature and character of God, the greater emphasis will always be in pointing back to the real article.

The unfortunate truth is that you may have a distorted view of God. If these cracks in your foundation are allowed to grow, everything that you build on them, which encompasses all of life, may crack and crumble. While there is no GPS system for where you must journey next, critical reflection and a revelation from the Holy Spirit will guide you as you seek a more proper understanding of the nature and character of God.

[For Personal Growth]

Spend some time reflecting on your early relationship with your parents. Do you see ways in which this relationship has shaped your foundational view of God?

If you had to guess, in what ways do you feel your view of God is cracked?

[With A Group]

Go around the group and share who your favorite "TV dad" was growing up. What made this character stand out to you?

As a group, read and discuss Colossians chapter 1.

What surprises you? What challenges you? What are you noticing for the first time? What stands out to you?

How does this understanding of Jesus challenge your existing view of God?

If there is time, share and discuss anything else from this chapter that challenged you.

Before you close in prayer, have each person share with the group what measurable and practical way you are going to respond to God this week.

[My Next Step]

[FOUR]

GOD vs THE COSMIC COP
Just the Facts, Ma'am.

> "My soul, you too must listen to the Word of God.
> Do not be foolish, do not let the din of your folly
> deafen the ears of your heart. For the Word
> Himself calls you to return."
> **Saint Augustine, *Confessions*, 81**

This story begins as I was driving my family back home to Colorado on New Year's Day of 2018. You'll see right away that this is not a particularly happy story, if for nothing else because I was driving through Kansas at the time. There truly may be nothing wrong with the state of Kansas, I have never lived there to say for sure, however, there is only so much a person can take when it comes to seeing the exact same scene of flat land and empty corn fields with one lone tree that is always out your right-hand window. I digress.

It was later in the evening at this point and for some time we had been the only vehicle on the road. While driving along, I soon spotted a vehicle that was non-conspicuously sitting in the median. Being as it was immediately obvious what this vehicle was, I dropped my speed a couple miles per hour - not because I was speeding, but just to be safe - and moved into the right-hand lane. As I gazed into my rear-view mirror, I saw the car begin to enter the highway… going in my direction.

In that moment, I had an immediate flashback to my earliest years as a licensed driver. My mind returned to my 16 to 18 year-old self. I think it was about the third or fourth time I had gotten pulled over within a two year span. Each time seemed more pointless than the last. The first time I got pulled over, it was for a tail light that had gone out. While this is a valid reason to pull someone over, I also just happened to be driving home from the store where I had quite literally just purchased a new bulb.

The second time I was pulled over in those formative driving years was for expired plates. Now, I will admit that I had indeed waited a bit too long on this one, but, once again, I had literally just picked up the new stickers from my grandparents house, where our mail went to in those days, and was going to apply them when I got home.

By the third time I was pulled over, I started to wonder if there wasn't actually some sort of notice that had gone out across Wyoming that was causing the police to target me or if I had somehow just won the lottery three times in a row. I would be okay being pulled over if I had been breaking a traffic law, but each time those lights flashed it seemed to be without much cause.

This time, I was told that my muffler was too loud. I concede that my '77 pickup truck wasn't in the best of shape. In fact, it was something of a Frankenstein already with a blue truck-bed having been attached to a white cab. The seats were thrown together, with two captains seats replacing the original bench seating and a wood table having been placed in the middle and skillfully attached to the floor for some reason. That wood bench had created something of a game for my friends. Since I was often the one driving, it became popular to "call wood," instead of calling "shotgun." Still, for all of its problems, I could not say that my Franken-truck was "disturbing the peace," especially since I had been pulled over on a busy street in the middle of the day.

I believe it was this string of what I considered to be silly run-ins with the law that led to my irrational fear of police officers when they were in their cruisers. As an unusually law-abiding citizen, I have little need to be watching over my shoulder for the long arm of the law.

Yet, as my wife will attest in frustration, if I see a police vehicle anywhere behind me, I begin to break out in an instant cold sweat. My hands immediately fly to 10 and 2, gripping the wheel as if I were on the final lap at Daytona. My mind begins racing. I become hyper-aware of the exact speed I am going, my lane placement, and the other vehicles around me. It is almost as if every one of my senses becomes supercharged for a moment in time.

Should the unfortunate occur and said police vehicle get behind me, I immediately begin looking for alternate routes to take. My eyes dart towards whatever the next exit is, thinking about how I can get off the road and still make it to my destination, without looking like I am ducking the law. In those moments, I almost immediately disconnect from any conversation I am having... just ask my wife. My focus moves to one thing, and one thing alone; where is that police officer and what is he or she doing?

It has been almost twenty years since I had that string of incidents where I was pulled over. Yet, that string of offenses, so early in my driving years, left what seems to be a permanent mark. It has left a distortion in my psyche as to the role that police play in the flow of moving vehicles. In actuality, police officers are there to serve and protect. But, don't even think about trying to tell me that when one is behind me in traffic! In those moments, they exist only to find something, even something small and insignificant, to pull me over for.

As we drove down that forsaken Kansas highway, this officer of the law seemed to be toying with me. After having left his cozy median, he immediately pulled in behind me. I prepared myself for the signature blue and red flashing lights, but they didn't come. Instead, the officer followed me for a while.

I was sure he was waiting for me to go just a little too fast, but I refused to bow to this game. Eventually, he pulled into the other lane and began to drive in such a way that he was just a half-car length behind being parallel to my mini-van. That's right, I have kids AND a mini-van. Extra nerd-dad points there.

This officer of the law repeated his pattern again. He moved back behind me, and I broke into a cold sweat and prepared for the inevitable. The lights didn't come. Instead, he moved back to driving beside me. This time, however, he sped up and drove ahead of me for a moment. It was at this point that I really started thinking about how I could get to the nearest exit and ditch this guy.

Suddenly, he hit his brakes and pulled back behind me once more. This time the lights turned on. At this point, I couldn't imagine what he had dreamed up to try to convict me of. I hadn't sped. I refused to play his lane-hopping game. Everyone in the car was wearing their seatbelts. All I could think about in that moment was how innocent I was, how evil this police officer was, and how justified I was in being paranoid when seeing police vehicles.

I pulled the mini-van over to the side of the road with great precision and gentle timing. I wasn't going to give this man any more to go on than whatever he had concocted in his corrupt mind. A quick tapping surprised us from my wife's passenger window. In spite of the fact that I was clearly far enough away from the road - I know, I immediately double and triple checked - for this man to come to the driver's side window as one would expect, he had chosen to go to the passenger side window.

Now my mind was racing even more. That's what cops do in drug busts. That's what corrupt cops do when they are going to try to pin something on you. Why else would this dastardly badge-wearing monster approach the passenger window. A flashlight beam crossed our faces. I began to panic a little. Slowly, with just enough delay that I could hit the gas if he drew his gun suddenly, I rolled down the window.

"Good evening," he said. Of course he would start with that line. That's what all mass murderers open with.

An uncomfortable silence filled the microseconds it took for my wife to calmly and kindly respond to this demon that was being highlighted by alternating red and blue lights. She didn't seem to fully understand in that moment that this person standing just inches from her was only being held back by the steal and fiberglass protecting her from being snatched up in his tentacles. Her kindness to this man only served to make me more upset and somehow more paranoid. A million lifetimes passed in front of my pre-frontal cortex in the momentary pause that, in retrospect, is simply natural conversational flow.

"Do you realize that your driver's side headlight is out?" The officer calmly and kindly said.

You've got to be kidding me. All of that anguish. All of that false demonization of a really good representation of our highway patrol. All of that white-knuckle chest pounding anticipation. I had been pulled over for a headlight being out. Worse yet, the officer was one of the nicest people I had met. Not only did he not ticket us, he gave us great tips on where to go in town at that hour to get a replacement so we wouldn't chance getting pulled over on the remainder of our trip back to Denver. Because of past experience that was uncritically processed and then compounded by years of growing paranoia, I had allowed myself to mischaracterize a great authority figure who simply had my best interests at heart. Sound familiar? Do you see where this is going?

This is where our discussion of possible distortions of the character of God will begin. In much the same way that I become unreasonable and paranoid when an officer of the law is driving behind me in traffic, many people see God as a "Cosmic Cop" who is just watching and waiting for them to do something wrong so He can "get" them. Even though this god smells an awful lot more like the Greek conception of Zeus, who sits in the sky hurling lightning bolts down upon those who don't bow to his every whim, this is a popular misconception of the true God of the universe. Many people mistakenly see God as "the Cosmic Cop."

Think critically for just a moment. When you think of God, do you think of a god who is simply waiting for you to screw up so that He can punish you? Do you imagine that with each offense you cause Him to suffer, that God is grinning from ear to ear as He grips the crackling lightning bolt of punishment and gleefully takes aim at your exact longitude and latitude on this terrestrial sphere?

Unfortunately, many people would, perhaps unknowingly, agree with this false caricature of the Almighty. Certainly, they argue, a good God who cannot condone sin in any form must punish such sin to the highest degree allowable and with such immediate accuracy that no human person could ever be free from the sting of His arrows. Even those who have not been trained by the stain of religion seem to have thoughts on some great karma in the universe that works so immediately and precisely that they find themselves in mortal danger with every real or imagined offense.

Here is the good news; this god does not exist. This is not God as He reveals Himself in the Bible. Further, it is actually dangerous to our faith to view God through this distorted and cloudy lens. Dr. Sanders has said, "No intimacy or relationship is ever established with someone whom you fear and wish only to keep from punishing you[9]."

The Bible does tell us that we are to fear God. In fact, it says that this is the beginning of true wisdom and understanding in life. However, were you to do an etymological study (a big word that simply means to uncover the origin and use of a particular word) on the very particular sense of the word used that we translate as "fear" and what nuance it has against the kind of fear that makes God look to us like the "boogeyman" looks to a four year old, and I believe you will come to a very different conclusion.

God is not the cosmic boogeyman. He isn't hiding in your closet, waiting to scare you. He does not threaten us with hushed and frightening tones that come from underneath our beds like Howie Mandel in *Little Monsters* or Pennywise from Stephen King's *It*.

Fearing God, in a Biblical sense, is about reverencing the One that is so far beyond what our imaginations can fathom. It includes an understanding that He is the Author and Finisher of all life. He *could* in His infinite power snuff out every atom in creation with a single thought. He wouldn't even need to snap His fingers (Thanos anyone?). All God would need to do is think and it would happen.

Fearing God does include recognizing that God is so much bigger, so much more and beyond anything we have ever thought about, dreamed up, or imagined in our most epic of fantasies. Fearing God does include wrestling with the truth that God created a planet that is both beautiful and terrifying all at once. That same planet that is filled with the unexplainable beauty of a field covered in butterflies also produces F5 tornadoes that rip through our meticulously built cities, inconveniently rearranging what so many have spent so much time and energy placing together in just that certain manner.

God is to be feared... but not in the way a 5 year-old fears a scary clown. While we all know that clowns just can't be trusted, there is something different about the character of God that we must come to understand to truly discover a proper and Biblical fear of Him.

In what may well be the earliest piece of writ in our entire Biblical history, a man named Job (pronounced like the guy off *Arrested Development*, not the place you draw a paycheck from) confronts God with a head and heart full of misinformation about Him. Job had a right to be a little angry considering everything he had ever built up was stripped from him in the most devastating series of events one could possibly imagine. Add to this the fact that Job's friends pretty much tell him that it is all because he is a sinner and it is all his fault. Then, add the fact that his own wife tells him to curse God and die, and you have quite the recipe for an... interesting... conversation with God.

Job confronts God directly, and God responds in the most unexpected manner, yet one that is entirely consistent with His magnificent character. God does what He always does, He meets Job exactly where he needed to be met and in just the right manner to which Job needed for God to meet Him. For multiple chapters God silences Job's questions with even greater questions. The conversation points us back to just how beyond our knowledge God really is as He points out who designed and created majestic horses, who laid the foundations of the earth, and who keeps the waters of the earth at bay, among other things.

Truly, to fear God IS the beginning of all wisdom. We must recognize that while God is entirely good, He is also capable of things we have not even begun to imagine in our wildest dreams, or in Hollywood's most esoteric fare. This type of fear, however, is NOT the same fear as the aforementioned scary clown archetype creates in us. We should not fear God as one fears an oncoming train. Both the scary clown and the oncoming train have suspect motives. As we come to understand God's true character, we do not see a galactic ax murderer who is simply awaiting His next unwitting victim. Neither do we see the cosmic cop who is waiting for us to miss the mark so he can pull out the eternal handcuffs.

It all comes back to the character of God. What sense of fear should we have for someone who is the very incarnation of love, joy, peace, patience, kindness, goodness, gentleness, faithfulness and self-control? It is not the same kind of fear we have for inanimate trains or imaginary clown-shaped bed bugs the size of spiders (sweet dreams).

Fear in the sense of the cosmic cop jails our relationship with the one true God and works to separate us from Him through iron bars. When we see God as out to get us, it is impossible to ever truly trust Him. This sort of fear creates an unsurpassable gulf between us and the Creator. This sort of fear never allows us to see His true nature and character, and instead creates only a false image that tries to con us into cowering before it. That sounds a lot more like a deceitful devil than a loving Creator.

So, am I saying that there is no cosmic punishment for wrong-doing? Am I negating the holiness of God (more on this aspect of our Creator later)?

Am I saying that God is not sovereign? Am I saying that sin should increase so that grace may also increase?

Once again, we must come back to the character of Who God really is. One aspect of this is that God is Creator. He designed all of life and the many systems that uphold and sustain the universe. God created life to work in certain ways, and to become hindered or to break when we choose to live counter to those wise ways.

The ancient Jewish world called this concept "wisdom." It was wisdom to live in such a way that you were working with how God designed life. It was "foolishness" to live life in such a way that you worked counter to God's best. Later on, once the Law was introduced, another layer was added in. It wasn't just foolish to live life counter to how our good and beautiful God created it to work, it was also sin.

Even the followers of Jesus get a little murky on the topic of sin these days. On the one hand, we argue, Jesus died on the cross for all sins and so we are free from the tether of the Law, which was only ever meant to be a handmaiden who led us to Christ. On the other hand, the followers of Jesus, who were directly impacted by His teachings, keep talking about the problem of sin.

For a moment, let's look at a powerful piece of God's Holy Word. We will also examine this same verse in the next chapter, but from a different perspective of focus.

Romans 8:12-17:

> "So then, brothers and sisters, we are not obligated to the flesh to live according to the flesh, because if you live according to the flesh, you are going to die. But, if by the Spirit you put to death the deeds of the body, you will live. For all those led by God's Spirit are God's sons. You did not receive a spirit of slavery to fall back into **fear**. Instead, you received the Spirit of **adoption**, by Whom we cry out, 'ABBA, Father!' The Spirit Himself testifies together with our spirit that we are God's children, and if children, also heirs - heirs of God and coheirs with Christ - if indeed we suffer with Him so that we may be glorified with Him" (Romans 8:12-17 CSB, emphasis added).

Notice the key words that I have highlighted in the text. We are not made for fear. We are not following the cosmic cop who will jail us for every perceived wrong. However, that doesn't mean, either, that right and wrong do not exist. Here, Paul shows us that there is a way of living that is purely from our "flesh," and a way of living that is guided by the Spirit of God. This harkens back to the Hebrew concept of wisdom and foolishness, but adds the game-changing dynamic of the Spirit of God.

We are God's children (more on this in the next chapter), therefore we are called to act like it. Sin still leads to death. The more we choose the flesh, the more we are choosing to break our relationship with God. He lays before us the choice between life and death, and He challenges us to choose life. Choosing life, however, means living with someone else at the center. We are no longer in charge, instead, we fearfully (in the proper sense of that word) lay our rights and preferences at the feet of Jesus and allow His Spirit to guide us.

When we choose to live by the Spirit and put to death our fleshly ways, we find life. It is our choices and the choices of others that this and other texts in Scripture affirm lead to what we would call the "good" or "bad" consequences of life.

Again, there are three wills in the universe. There is God's perfect will, which leads to life. There is our will, which Scripture tells us we can conform to the Spirit or allow to be malformed by the flesh. There is also the will of the enemy, who comes to steal, kill and destroy.

There are consequences for our actions and choices. This isn't karma. It's not about input = output. However, there is a Biblical law of reaping and sowing. When we sow to the flesh, we reap the pains of sin. When we sow to the Spirit, we reap the fullness of life. There are much greater works on the differences between retributive karma and the Biblical law of reaping and sowing. I'll not dive much deeper than that. If for nothing else, karma is a cold and impersonal force that does not account for the personal and unreasonable grace and mercy of God.

What we must take away from this, then, is the following. Yes, our choices have consequences, sometimes even eternal ones. No, this does not mean that God is watching us with glee as He prepares a cracked whip. We are not called to have a spirit of fear, because we understand the character of our good and beautiful God. Instead, we are called to live like His sons and daughters. His grace has paid the price for our sins and it is this prevenient grace that allows us to become more

31

like Him. Therefore, God sets before us a choice, life being guided by His Spirit, or seeing the consequences built into sin when we live by our flesh.

If seeing God as the cosmic cop is a misrepresentation of His character, then how should we understand God? Isn't there some term Jesus gives us to refer back to God that would help us better understand how He shaped life to work for our good and why He asks us to avoid the stain of sin?

Perhaps there is.

[For Personal Growth]

Read Romans 8:12-17 at least three times. Note any word, phrase, or idea that sticks out to you.

What is God trying to say to you through this?

Being honest with yourself, have you primarily seen God as out to get you or as a cosmic cop?

How is this understanding a misconception of God's character?

[With A Group]

Group material resumes at the end of the next chapter. Read both chapters prior to discussion.

[My Next Step]

[FIVE]

GOD AS FATHER
He Who Must Not Be Named.

> "It is… not that there is first of all human fatherhood
> and then a so-called divine fatherhood, but
> just the reverse; true and proper fatherhood
> resides in God and from this fatherhood
> what we know as fatherhood among us
> men is derived."
> **Karl Barth**

I really didn't know my father growing up. I mean, I knew he existed and guessed that he probably had some sort of love for me, but I didn't *know* him. I caught glimmers and shadows of him here and there, but never really experienced the fullness of his presence. When I was very young, my mom and I would run into him around town every once in a while, and it was always very cordial. He would tell me how big I had gotten and promise something; a toy, an adventure, a go-kart. I really wanted that go-kart. I mean I *really* wanted that go-kart. What happened when I got it that almost led Taiwan to sue my grandfather and break diplomatic relations with the state of Wyoming is, however, a story for another time.

When I was in Jr. High and had started going to church, I was surprised to see my dad one day in the church building. This wasn't a Sunday, so I didn't understand why he was there. Frankly, I had never seen him there on Sunday, either. It turns out, he had been hired to work on the new gym area the church was building. For a few moments, we talked.

Then, there was that Easter that dad randomly showed up at our house and stayed the night on the couch. I didn't know exactly what was going on that day, but I had seen enough spy movies to make some guesses as my mother and father (two words I don't know I've really ever used in the same sentence) sat me down and explained to me that dad was going to sleep on the couch, he had a gun under the cushions, just in case, and I was not to go near the gun or open the door to anyone that night. But, then, just like a vapor, dad was gone again. I would later discover that he had moved to Arizona, and that was that. The story doesn't pick up again until I was studying for my Master's Degree in Kentucky and my father began writing me from prison.

Growing up, I had convinced myself that it was somehow better that dad wasn't around. Mom made sure never to bad-mouth him to me, but I had figured out pretty early on that he was not going to be reliable in my life and had also known of some of the bad things he had gotten himself into.

I knew that my father was using drugs and had more than a bit of a taste for alcohol, as well. I reasoned to myself that it was better that I didn't know my father and pick up these traits from him. I knew that I also have a bit of an addictive tendency, so I figured that perhaps I was being spared by not having him in my life.

It wasn't until I was in college, studying to be a pastor, that this facade began to crumble. In what was a very unexpected season, I found myself being challenged by multiple different sources to consider what I would later learn to define as an "absent father wound." Turns out, God wanted to do some healing in my heart in that season of life. While I don't believe that God micromanages the universe, I do believe it was more than coincidence that so many things in my life began to point me back to dear ol' dad.

It all started with the very lesson that this chapter contains, which I was taught in my freshman year of college in the class *Biblical Life and Witness*. The second, more unexpected source, was found in the TV show my roommates and I decided was going to be "our show." At the end of each day, after having gone to classes and/or work, we would turn on the then-currently-new adventures of Superman via the CW's teen-angst-filled *Smallville*. In the first few seasons of the show, a teenaged Clark Kent begins wrestling with the reality that his real father abandoned him, all the while learning to embrace the fatherhood of the man who raised him.

The trifecta was completed by a book some of my friends and I decided to study called *Wild At Heart*. In this modern classic, author John Eldredge points the reader back to, among other things, the absent father wound many of us bear and shows just how much this wound impacts us deep into our old age if we do not address it.

I remember clearly, after one episode of *Smallville* that was particularly hammering home young Clark's father-wound, walking out of our dorm room and wandering off into the little wooded area beside our school. I remember looking up into the sky and realizing just how deeply this absent father wound was impacting me. In class, we had learned that our view of God is shaped by our early relationship with our earthly father. I knew this to be true as I reflected on my own life.

In all honesty, even though I was studying to be a pastor, God seemed an awful lot like my absent dad. He was out there, somewhere. He acknowledged my existence, of which He was largely responsible for. He probably cared about me, most likely. Maybe He even loved me in His own way... but, He wasn't there. He wasn't accessible. I couldn't call out to him and get an answer. I only saw Him in glimpses and shadows, never in His fullness. When I did call out to Him, He might pay some attention, but likely had other things in His life going on that would keep Him from answering my call.

That was an incredibly accurate depiction of how I really saw God deep down, even if my... ahem... espoused theology (a fancy way to say what I said I believed about God) differed greatly from this. I knew that wasn't truly the nature and character of God... but the wound was deep. It was deeper than I had ever imagined. I could say with my lips that I was better off not having grown up with a dad all I wanted... It simply wasn't true. I was wounded. I was without an earthly dad... and this wound deeply impacted how I saw God. However, as I would come to learn, I was never fatherless.

It was in that difficult and beautiful season of life that God, just as Eldredge said needed to happen, opened up my puss-filled wound like a careful and loving doctor. It was in that season that He began cutting deeper than I would have ever felt comfortable with, but this was exactly what had to happen. I needed that wound opened. I needed to be taken back to the source of the pain. I had been trying to apply topical ointment to an infection that was much more than skin-deep. It was only in the depth of that wound that God could begin the healing.

There is a lot more to that story than I have space here to elucidate upon. My dad ended up in federal prison. There, he recommitted his life to Jesus. He began writing me regularly. Then, a series of God-moments started happening. First, there was a prison riot that saw my dad be moved to Oklahoma, only an hour from where I lived. There, dad met my wife and we began to reconnect a bit as a family. Once he got out of prison (the second time), he eventually landed a job hauling freight. As providence would have it, his route for a couple years went from Texas to about an hour outside of Columbus, Ohio, where I was living at that time. It was in this season that dad got to know my son a bit.

God is still telling that story. It has some new chapters that went in unexpected directions, but I don't get the sense that it is done just yet. Even with dad back in the picture for a season, that wound wasn't healed overnight. It wasn't fixed the first, second, or third time I read *Wild At Heart*. It wasn't even fixed by the tenth and final season of *Smallville*. In that season, God began to do something in my heart and soul that I am forever grateful for. He began to re-Father me. God had to open the wound I protected so fiercely in order to show me that I was never truly fatherless. God was and is my true father.

Who is this God Person, *Anyway?*

I don't think it is any mistake that Jesus' favorite way to refer to God is "Father." We can debate long into the night about the reality that God is neither male or female in the way that we think of things. In fact, the Bible specifically says that both male and female are made in the image of God. God is not limited by the boundaries of gender in the ways that we think about them, as gender itself is a created construct by a gender-full God from which both man and woman find their identity. A whole other book could be written on that loaded subject. Still, God did distinctly create male and female and did purposefully pour aspects of His image into each.

We could also argue long into the day that the culture of Jesus' day was highly patristic; that is, male-centered and male-dominated. In Jesus' day and age, women were considered low-level property that belonged to their husbands or fathers. Perhaps, we astutely reason, this is why Jesus used the male term "Father," instead of the then less culturally hierarchical term "mother." Certainly, there are several places in Scripture where God is referred to in a more "motherly" manner. However, this argument doesn't really hold up either, as Jesus was VERY bold to correct any place society or religion did not line up with the Kingdom of God.

Jesus broke all of the rules when it came to empowering women, setting captives free, redefining religion, speaking out for the oppressed, breaking down the walls between Jew and Gentile, fulfilling the Jewish law and yet moving humanity out from the power of it and into the power of the Spirit. Jesus told the religious that while they were focused on the external, He was focused on the internal. He redefined their view of why the Sabbath was created. He told them that even looking at a woman with lust in their hearts was the same as throwing her down publicly and engaging in sexual acts with her. Jesus spent a whole lot of His ministry helping people redefine the misconceptions they had about God, the Kingdom of God, eschatology (the study of the end of the world), the work of the Spirit, and so, so, so, so, so, so much more.

It's not like the idea of God as Father was hidden during His ministry, either. It's not as if the Pharisees and other religious leaders didn't bring the topic up. It's not as if Jesus avoided the topic. There's that whole scene where He is 12 and says, "Didn't you know I would be in my **Father's** house?" Don't you think that if the God-as-Father meta-narrative needed adjusting, that Jesus would speak boldly to mankind about how it had gotten off-center and adjust it?

Actually, He did.

In fact, one of the most revolutionary things Jesus ever did was tell people they could relate to God as Father. To fully understand this, we need to set the scene. 1st Century. Middle-East. Devoted followers of God who were handpicked as His people, known as the Jews. Among these Jews, the most dedicated and most devoted religious persons perhaps ever to have lived; the pharisees.

We know from Scripture that the Pharisees followed Jesus all over the place. They were present at many, perhaps most, maybe all of Jesus' major teachings. These religious leaders, in their attempt to ensure that God's name was kept holy as the Decalogue (a fancy way of referring to "The Ten Words" or Ten Commandments) prescribes, would not write out or even say the name of God. This is why in your English Bible the word

"LORD" is often used in all caps and/or italics to indicate that another word once existed there.

You see, in order to not profane the name of God, scholars and scribes would regularly omit God's name from the text. They would sometimes use the appellation "Adoni," in its place. They would sometimes simply leave the word blank. This practice often also carried over into their pattern of speech. Rather than say the name of God out loud, they would simply leave an audible pause and then add, "may His name be praised." Some still abide by this practice, writing G-d instead of God.

In the world in which Jesus physically lived as fully God become fully man, to refer to God with any particular word or phrase from unholy and unclean lips was to risk somehow contaminating His precious and holy name, thus breaking at least two of the big Ten Commandments, along with perhaps a few rules these leaders had created themselves. If these religious leaders, who had much societal sway over the day-to-day life and habits of the nation of Israel, felt so strongly about this "not saying God's name" thing, then the people would, as well.

Enter Jesus.

Jesus had a habit of calling God "Father." Think about it. How does the very prayer Jesus told us to pray begin? "Our Father..." Flying in the face of religion, Jesus told common man that we have a true Father and can relate to God as Father. Not only can we say His name with our lips and with our pens, we can call Him by a word that has a very specific meaning when tied to earthly terms.

But, even this isn't quite the fullness of what Jesus actually said.

You see, the word that Jesus often used was "Abba." Abba was the word an Aramaic child of that day would use to refer to their male earthly progenitor, but it doesn't mean "Father" in the strictest of senses. This isn't the word you would use if you were trying to be prim and proper in your Victorian etiquette. This isn't a term religious people would ever be comfortable with in the slightest. It was simply too informal and too personal.

In truth, "abba" was the word a young child, barely fresh into their existence, would spit out as they toddled towards their dad with their little chunky arms extended, drool cascading like Niagara from their round and rosy cheeks. The closest equivalent we have in our language isn't "father," it's not "dad," or even "daddy." The closest word we have to "abba" is "dada." This is the simplistic minimalistic utterance that a little baby gleefully coos as they look up into the eyes of their loving father while they try to come up with a way to personalize and contextualize him through their lack of language and untrained little baby mouths.

One of the most revolutionary things Jesus ever did was to tell a world that was so afraid that their carefully crafted words might somehow fall short and profane the name of God that they could refer to Him in the same way a child does as it is learning to mumble before it can even talk. Brennan Manning notes of this term that "Jewish children used this intimate colloquial form of speech in addressing their fathers... As a term for divinity, however, it was unprecedented not only in Judaism but in any of the great world religions[10]." Notice his insight here, not only was this uncomfortable for the religious, it was **unprecedented** in the history of religion to refer to God in such an intimate and vulnerable way.

Manning further notes, "a central theme in the personal life of Jesus Christ, which lies at the very heart of the revelation that He is, is His growing intimacy with, trust in, and love of His Abba... Herein lies the great novelty of the Gospel. Jesus, the beloved Son, does not hoard this experience for Himself. He invites and calls us to share this same intimate and liberating relationship[11]."

This practice didn't stop with Jesus, either. His early followers seem to have caught the "dada" bug, as well. In his masterful letter to the Romans, the Apostle Paul, who was a direct witness of the great power of Jesus, both comforts and confronts his readers with the following words in Romans 8:12-17:

> "So then, brothers and sisters, we are not obligated to the flesh to live according to the flesh, because if you live according to the flesh, you are going to die. But, if by the Spirit you put to death the deeds of the body, you will live. For all those led by God's Spirit are God's sons. You did not receive a spirit of slavery to fall back into fear. Instead, you received the Spirit of adoption, by Whom we cry out, '**ABBA**, Father!' The Spirit Himself testifies together with our spirit that we are God's children, and if children, also heirs - heirs of God and coheirs with Christ - if indeed we suffer with Him so that we may be glorified with Him" (Romans 8:12-17 CSB, emphasis added).

Notice how Paul, an apostle of Jesus, redefines life around our identity as children of God. Notice, further, how Paul refers to God as abba. Context is always incredibly important when reading any text, and most especially when reading Scripture. In this case, understanding a little of the context of who this author is brings some incredible insights. Paul wasn't just a Jew. Paul wasn't just a highly religious Jew. Paul was a pharisee. Paul was one of the very people who would have sternly upheld the law of God and made sure that no unclean thing could ever misrepresent God, even killing to make sure no defilement could come from unclean lips.

Notice the amazing language that Paul uses. "You did not receive a spirit of slavery to fall back into fear. Instead, you received the Spirit of adoption, by whom we cry out, 'ABBA, Father!'" This text does not point to an impersonal force, but to a life-giving Spirit. It is "by Whom," not by what. Notice also that this Spirit does not lead us into slavery and fear. When we come to God, we do not come to the cosmic cop. We should not fear God in the punitive sense.

Instead, and this may be the most important concept you could ever read in rebuilding your firm foundation, we receive a Spirit of adoption! We are not God's unwilling slaves, we are His chosen and redeemed children. We are His dearly loved sons and daughters bought with an unimaginable price which repaid the debt of sin, defeated the grave, and gave us the ability and inward compulsion to cry out "ABBA, Father!"

God isn't interested in us fearing Him in a way that we put Him behind glass and make sure that no impurity of ours ever stains the masterpiece. God wants us to relate to Him as His dearly loved children. That is mind-bending. That is astonishing. That was unheard of, invasive, and culture changing to its originally intended audience, and it should be just as invasive and culture changing for us. This was a stick of dynamite held tightly in the hand of man-made religion, and it still has the power to blow our hearts wide-open, right where we are in our man-made cages that we often willing enter into and call day-to-day life.

This is really important stuff. It is all too easy from our modern lens to look back on this text and be unimpressed. We need to understand that these words were like a burning fire to the original readers. These words drew people in from the cold and caused them to snuggle up to a strange warmth they didn't yet understand. They caused amazement and awe. It is unfortunate that we have lost the awe and wonder this text and this concept produces.

But, I get it. I understand that disconnect.

When I first laid eyes on my son as he exited his previous address in my wife's womb, it was the most astonishing thing I had ever imagined. I looked in wide-eyed wonder at his little toes, his little fingers, and even his really oddly shaped head. It's not that his head was weird or anything, it's just that all babies have really oddly shaped heads if they come out the natural way into the outside world.

In that first moment of his life, right as he was being laid upon my wife's chest, I said, "hey there buddy." He literally lifted his head up at a full-tilt, turned his face towards me, and smiled. I honestly didn't think that feat was possible with little floppy baby necks, but it happened. It happened and it caused a sense of wonder to rise up in me that I had never before felt. That was a moment I would never forget.

Yet, as I have spent more and more time in the presence of my son, I have become less in awe of his fingers and toes. Especially, at the age of six now, when he uses them to stomp off and cross his arms in a huff. I have become less enamored by the raising of his head, though I am often surprised when he lifts his head away from YouTube Kids before we tell him his time on that platform is up. I love my son. He still amazes me on a regular basis. It's just that what once awed me slowly became familiar.

The longer you are with someone or something, the less you focus on what caused awe in you in the first place. When we come to Scripture's portrait of the true and living God, we are confronted by a God who is consistent with the revelation of father. Yet, these words no longer shock us as they did when Jesus was first uttering them. We've heard them all our life. If they shock us, now, it's because culture has shifted to a point where the concept of referring to God in male terms now seems insensitive or even hurtful.

The word "father" is often hard to hear through our modern ears. As mentioned previously, we live in a world where fatherlessness is unfortunately more common than it is for someone to have had a good experience with their earthly father. As such, understanding the love of a good father is entirely foreign to many.

We also live in a world where the strength of men has been abused for so long that we fear (in the scary clown sense) any man who shows strength or power, instantly grouping them in the same category that I still wrongly group police officers when they are behind me in traffic. Men are just too much of a danger to be trusted. We instantly assume that a strong male is to be punished, not praised in today's world.

As Philipps has said, "...the early conception of God is almost invariably founded upon the child's idea of his father[12]." Unfortunately, it is more likely than not that you have a bad taste in your mouth for the word "father." However, we must understand what we are doing. We are taking our conception of our earthly fathers, including their failures that we know all too intimately, and extrapolating that image onto God.

When I say that God is consistent with the revelation of Father, I do not mean that you should look to your earthly father's imperfections and wrongly place them on God. Instead, wherever the goodness and love of our fathers have brought healing and life, that is borrowed character from the one True father.

As James Bryan Smith has said in his masterful work *The Good and Beautiful God*, "When Jesus describes God as Father, we have to let Him define what fatherhood means... God as Father and Jesus as Son existed before any human father and son (or daughter) existed. Therefore, fatherhood is first defined by God and Jesus, not by Adam and his children[13]." Smith goes on to add, "Many people... have been deeply wounded by their biological fathers, and this makes thinking about God as Father very difficult. The solution is not to abandon the term father, but to let Jesus define it[14]."

God is the perfect Father. God treats us the way a perfect father would treat children that He desperately loves. He does not punish us for the joy of punishing us. He does not wait for us to screw up so He can "get" us. As our perfect Father, God believes in us. He wants the best for us. He does not force us to obey, but holds out the Word of Life. He gives us the path to walk that leads to life, and through His Spirit and grace allows us to walk it in spite of the stain our sin once left.

He is there with us, helping us, working with us so we can become more and more like Him. He allows us to experience the weight of our consequences, yet also helps us to grow through them and become more fully alive as a result. He doesn't strip us of our identity, instead He provides the framework of our soul and leads us to become more like what we were created to be. He helps us become the best version of ourselves by becoming more like His perfect character. God believes in us. God fights for us. God sings over us.

Smith's powerful words resonate in my soul. I was fatherless. Yet, God wanted to show me that He was, is, and always will be my true father. I had to enter into that absent father wound and feel the weight of my loss. I had to stop pretending that I was better for not having had an earthly father who was present in my life. I needed God to show me what Jesus meant when He called God Father. And, I'm willing to bet you need that too. Even if you had a good father growing up who was there for you, they weren't perfect.

It's time to reclaim our hope in the Fatherhood of God. If you haven't asked God to re-Father you, perhaps it is time. Whether or not you knew your earthly father. Whether or not your earthly father brought good things into your life. It is time to turn back to God with one simple cry in our heart. I believe the questions and exercises for this chapter will be particularly powerful for you. I encourage you not to skip them.

Perhaps your heart needs to join my heart in its deep cry.

"Dada.

Father me!"

[For Personal Growth]

Read Romans 8:12-17 at least three times. On your final read through, pause with each phrase and listen for what God is saying to you.

What promises stand out to you in this set of verses?

[With A Group]

As a group, read and discuss Romans 8:12-17.

What surprises you? What challenges you? What are you noticing for the first time? What stands out to you?

How has your view of God been more like the cosmic cop misconception?

How has your relationship, or lack thereof, with your earthly father shaped your view of God?

What would it look like for God to "re-father" you?

As time allows, share and discuss anything from these two chapters that challenged you.

[My Next Step]

[SIX]

GOD vs THE ANCIENT MUMMY OF PHARAOH
This Place is Cursed.

> "Sir, my concern is not whether God is on
> our side; my greatest concern is to be on
> God's side, for God is always right."
> **Abraham Lincoln**

Back when Dr. Cliff Sanders was serving as a pastor in a local church, rather than as Chair of the Biblical Studies department of Mid-America Christian University as he does now, he would do what many pastors are called to do and visit the sick in the hospital. In that time, it was common for Pastors to make routine visits to the hospital and even visit and pray over those who were not a part of their own church.

On one of these particular days, Dr. Sanders introduced himself to a nice, yet clearly sick, young man. Once Cliff announced his status as a member of the clergy and his intention to pray, the man's face soured.

"I don't believe in God," the man proclaimed with disgust.

There must have been something telling in the way the man said that. There must have been some emotion that crossed his face. It could just be that Cliff Sanders is one of the most up-front people I have ever met. Whatever the reason, Cliff did not miss a single beat before asking this bed-ridden man the following:

"Really? Why don't you tell me about the god you don't believe in."

This was all the man needed to begin tearing into "god." For several minutes he described a god who is out to get us, who causes nations to go to war, who slaughters babies, who causes us pain every single time we make the wrong decision. This man let loose and laid bare his feelings about the god who was responsible for the holocaust, for mothers who lose their babies in tragic accidents, and who causes global warming all at once.

Dr. Sanders listened as this man ripped God from stem to sternum. When he was finished with his tirade, the man simply sat back with a smirk. It was fairly obvious he was proud of what he had accomplished. It was clear that this man felt very good about the opportunity that had presented itself to straighten up this foolish pastor. Certainly, he must have thought there was nothing this preacher-man could say other than to stammer over some words and excuse himself from the room.

This man didn't know Cliff Sanders, however. This is the same Cliff Sanders who stared down the feared biker gang known as the Banditos while living in Houston, Texas. For a moment, Cliff let the man have his win. He allowed the thick air to clear out of the room for a just a second. Then, Cliff responded.

"I don't believe in that god, either," he said, as the man in the hospital bed's face quickly turned from victory to confusion. "In fact," he added, "no sane person would believe in a god like you just described."

"What?" The man was now very concerned and confused as to how his perfect tirade was beginning to unravel.

"You didn't prove that you don't believe in God. You just proved that you're not stupid... that you have a brain in your skull."

Suddenly, this man was very interested in what this bold preacher had to say next. For the next few minutes, Dr. Sanders began to tell this man about the TRUE God. A God who is consistent with the revelation of Father. A God who is consistent with the person of Jesus Christ. A God who has our best interests at heart.

I don't know if that man came to know Jesus that day or not. What I do know is he likely never forgot the preacher who pointed his finger at him and told him he wasn't stupid and that he had a brain in his skull. Like this man in his hospital bed, we all have so much to unpack when it comes to the incorrect and non-Biblical things we tend to believe about God. If we were honest with ourselves, we're probably not far from this man in what we try to hide in our mental closets.

Try this exercise. Take a piece of paper or a journal and start to write out everything you actually, or even just might, believe about God. Do you believe He created the universe? Do you believe He causes natural disasters? Do you believe He, like Santa Claus, sees you when you're sleeping and knows when you're awake? Do you believe God is powerful, somewhat powerful, or all-powerful? Can God hear our thoughts? When we make a mistake, what sort of actions does God take for or against us? Ask yourself these and other questions.

Take some real time and write out whatever comes to mind. It may be simple one-word responses. You may write out full sentences or paragraphs. Maybe, if you're more an artistic mind, you'll need to draw pictures. Whatever it is that works for you, try to be as complete as possible. You might even surprise yourself at what comes to mind.

In all honesty, some people are likely not that far off in their conception of God from men like Stephen Fry who proclaimed in an interview that he has an answer for anyone who says they believe in a good God; "Cancer in babies... really?" We may not be that far from some intelligent thinkers like comedian Penn Jillette, who told Big Think that if you want to become an atheist, all you have to do is read the Bible. Penn had the unfortunate experience of attending a Congregationalist church in his youth where it was not okay to question God and ask about tough truths.

For many, if not most of us, we have some skeletons in the closet when it comes to our view of God. Whether through uncritically reflecting on life, passively accepting what we have heard from people on TV, blindly accepting what we heard from a pulpit, or whether through experiences that happened to us that we couldn't make sense of; most of us have allowed mischaracterizations of God to shape our view and understanding of Him.

Each of us need a Cliff Sanders in our life to tell us that when we say we don't believe in a god who would give cancer to babies that we're not stupid. We have a brain in our skulls. After all, does God give cancer to babies, or is it corporations who pollute our food, water, and air in the name of big bucks? It's nice to hear once in a while that when we doubt an evil, maleficent, malfeasant thing that some call god that we are not crazy. In fact, not only are we sane, we might just be closer to the truth than we realize.

I have heard many well-meaning believers say, "I know I shouldn't doubt God..." My response is usually, "why?" Job did. In spite of the fact that he was perhaps the greatest man of God in his time, he doubted God when great tragedy struck. John the Baptist doubted Jesus, his own cousin Whom he had publicly proclaimed as the long-awaited Messiah, when he sent a group of his followers to ask Jesus if He was really the One Israel had been awaiting. Jesus said that of those born of women there was perhaps no one greater than John the Baptist, yet when he found himself in prison and likely going to die, he doubted.

This may have been a trait John got from his father, Zechariah, a priest who was also considered a great man of God. When an angel came and told him that he and his wife would bear a child in their old age, Zech doubted. Actually, Zecariah might be a perfect study in the difference in doubt and unbelief, especially considering the consequences he faced for disbelieving what God was saying would happen. This is doubly so when you look at the similarities in Zech's story and Mary's story. Both are told something fantastic, one seems to have a healthy "how is this going to happen" doubt, the other seems to live in unbelief in that moment. It seems John the Baptist didn't fall far from his father's tree.

King David doubted God. Reading through the Psalms is not only an emotional roller-coaster, but a spiritual one, as well. In one moment you see David questioning to the point of doubt what God is up to in the extreme circumstances that he would face. Then, by the end of that same Psalm he will come back to the glory and goodness of God. The Bible says that David is a man after God's own heart, yet he had strong moments of doubt that he felt like putting to song.

In their Fuller Youth Institute (FYI) research project that was later published as the book *Growing Young*, Kara Powell, Jake Mulder, and Brad Griffin discovered the role that honest questions, sometimes presenting themselves in the form of doubt have to play in the healthy faith development of young people. "While fewer young people in our study are talking about faith with nonbelievers than we might hope, one of the characteristics most significantly related to gospel sharing is increased honesty about questions and struggles. Perhaps it's not *certainty* that makes young people better evangelists, but *honesty*[15]."

When it comes to developing a healthy faith, doubt isn't the enemy. In the aforementioned FYI study, Fuller discovered something so powerful that they turned it into a mantra for themselves. "It's not doubt that's toxic to faith. It's silence[16]." Their studies confirm something deep and challenging for us all. Doubts should not be seen as off-limits if we want to seriously follow God. In fact, if we are to follow God, healthy doubt is a part of the path we must walk. This isn't to say that we never resolve these doubts, far from it, but, they suggest, if we feel that we are not allowed to express our doubts, they will **never** get resolved.

As such, we should not see doubt as the enemy of faith. Instead, we need to begin to see doubt for what it can be. Doubt, when allowed to be expressed and worked through in a safe and caring environment where Jesus is proclaimed, can become "faith-forming opportunities rather than freak-out moments of failure[17]." Doubt isn't the opposite of faith. Doubt, when processed critically, can and will become a springboard to true faith. We must also come to understand that there is a difference between doubt and unbelief. Doubt is healthy, it can lead us to seek the truth. Unbelief, however, happens when truth is clear and we go the other way.

At the start of every one of our Life Groups at the church where I serve as pastor, small group leaders are encouraged to read through our "Guidelines for a Safe Group." Sitting among this short list of guidelines that are intended to help people discover Jesus and how He is invading and reshaping their story, is the imperative that "doubts are welcome." We feel that church should not be a place where doubts are off limits. That tends to have disastrous effects. Instead, church should be the place where honest doubts are free to be expressed, explored, and worked through as we all become more like Jesus each and every day.

Scripture itself commends those who take what is said, whether on the news, from a friend, by an "expert," or even from the pulpit and test it against Biblical truth. In Acts 17:11, we are told about the Bereans. Here it says, "the people here were of more noble character than those in Thessalonica, since they received the word with eagerness and examined the Scriptures daily to see if these things were so" (CSB).

Notice what is said of these Bereans. First of all, they are commended as having noble character. What context do we have that shows how their character was noble? They "eagerly" received what the apostles were telling them. In other words, they were excited to talk about God. They were excited to learn new truth. Being eager to understand more about life, the universe, and everything is a noble trait. However, their eagerness was also tempered with wisdom, which was another highly noble trait they showed. They would take everything that the apostles, the very men who were trained by Jesus, said and test it against the Scriptures. God considers an honest faith quest, even with doubts in play, to be a noble quest.

So, then, let's be noble. It is time to doubt another possibly imprecise view of God to see whether it lines up with the words of Scripture. One more misconception of God, that no sane person should ever believe in is the caricature I like to call "the Ancient Mummy of Pharaoh." Perhaps you've seen a movie or two with the word "mummy" in the title. A little less than half of them are worth watching. This view of God happens when we repress ideas about who God might be, entombing them like a wrapped-up mummy deep in our minds.

By many accounts, the pharaohs were unrelenting taskmasters who punished their servants/slaves past their point of breaking. They cared little to nothing for their well-being. Should their servants get sick or become unable to work, pharaoh simply tells them to get back up and put their bones to the grindstone or risk a fate worse than death.

In the same way, many people have this repressed idea about God that He is really an unrelenting taskmaster. He sees each of us as servants, maybe even slaves, and He will push us until He gets what He wants out of us. No matter what task has been accomplished and no matter what good we have done for Him, or for the world, there is always a fresh one waiting at the end of a cracked whip. This is the god of 110%.

Perhaps you've played on a sports-ball team at some point in your life where a hard-nosed coach gruffly told you that he/she expects nothing less than 110%. When you got out to practice, this coach forced you to run farther than you felt your spaghetti-legs could withstand. This person then had you embark on your (insert sports-ball-specific training of your choosing here) until your sweat was sweating sweat of its own.

After all of this preparation, you started doing runs, plays, base hits, free throws, curls, or whatever your sport of choosing focused on. You were already exhausted to the point of fainting, yet you knew that if you missed that shot, goal, basket, or calculation that you would receive no pity from coach. In fact, if you didn't do everything perfectly, you would be forced to run even more laps. Worse yet, if you missed that shot, coach would punish everyone on the team by making them run while you were not allowed to move; thus causing you to be a target later on in the locker room.

A person who sees God in this manner never feels like he or she is enough, no matter what they do. No matter what task is accomplished, there is always another one waiting at the end of a cracked whip. In this person's mind, his or her worth before God is based upon what they can do and it lasts only as long as they can continue to produce. Once they are unable to "do," God no longer has any use for them, and, like the depiction of ancient Egyptian rulers in the movies, this god will punish them before simply casting them to their doom.

The pharaoh god demands more than we can ever give and will never understand why we are unable to comply. When your ability to serve ends, this god will abandon you and leave you to find your end. Worse yet, perhaps this Ancient Mummy of Pharaoh, should he find you no longer of use, will land the killing blow himself.

Does this misconception of God ring true with you? Do you feel as though you can never do enough to please God? Do you know deep down that God is always asking for more than you have? Does it upset you when you think about this god and all you give in its name without so much as a pat on the back?

What if I told you this god doesn't exist?

If Scripture is true, there is nothing we can do to earn favor with the One True God. This is so counter to what we are told in life. Literally every religion in the world has a very simple equation of do = favor. They say doing is what saves us. Our actions are what earn good in life and peace in eternity. Whether it is "achieving" nirvana, "earning" favor, "going" clear, or "receiving" heaven as a "reward," many of us serve some form of the Ancient Mummy of Pharaoh and attempt to work our way into a good life and an even better afterlife.

However, like the Bereans, we must test this against the Word of God. In Ephesians 2:8-10 we see this mind-warping truth from God's heart. "For you are saved **by grace through faith**, and this is not from yourselves; it is God's gift - **not from works**, so that no one can boast. For we are His

workmanship, created in Christ Jesus for good works, which God prepared ahead of time for us to do" (CSB, emphasis added).

The Word of God tells us clearly that we cannot work to earn God's favor. Just as He is not standing with a lightning bolt ready to fry us when we do something wrong, neither do our attempts to do good earn us favor. God is not standing with leathery bronze arms that have been tempered by the Egyptian sun and holding a coiled whip, nor is He handing out participation trophies and extra credit.

Unlike every religion ever, the truth of Jesus is that there is simply not one thing we can do to earn eternity or favor with God. In fact, in the Old Testament prophetic book of Isaiah, we are told that our attempts at righteousness are like dirty, bloody, used menstrual cloths before God (see Isaiah 64:6). As we look through Scripture we do not see a god who whips us to work, we see the God who cares for us, first.

The word translated as "workmanship" in this verse is the Greek word poema. That word should look a little familiar to you, as it is where we get our English word "poem." What this text is saying is that we are God's poem, His masterpiece. We were composed line by line, on purpose, beautifully handcrafted by the greatest Poet/Creator ever. Far from facing a cracked whip, Scripture tells us that God sings His joy over us even when we are unaware (see Zephaniah 3:17). He is so deeply in love with us that His love cannot be measured in planets or stars.

Notice, though, that the text does tell us we are created to do good works. So, are we merely dealing with a more cuddly pharaoh god? No. To some it may simply look like a different starting point, sure, but WHAT a different starting point. We are created to do good WORKS… but, not at the end of a cracked whip. The starting point makes all of the difference. You see, unlike religion which tells us that we must earn god's favor, the One True God tells us that we already have His favor. We are His specially created children, His perfectly crafted sonnet. God sings exultantly in joy over us. It is from this basis of existing acceptance, empowerment, and love that we are then compelled to do good things.

You see, what comes first really does matter. If we start with works to earn acceptance, favor, merit, or eternity, then we have found ourselves bowing to an Ancient Mummy that was long ago placed dead in a tomb and wrapped in linen strips that form a wall against us. However, when we understand that in Jesus we are already accepted, loved, and empowered and from this foundation feel compelled to do good works and spread His love, then we may have just found the One True God.

Speaking of Jesus....

[For Personal Growth]

Read Ephesians 2:8-10 several times.

What does it mean that we can't earn heaven?

Why, then, are we created for good works?

How have you fallen back into the trap of trying to earn your way to God?

How do you react to Isaiah's shocking statement that these attempts are like dirty menstrual cloths to God?

What is the true basis of salvation, then?

[With A Group]

Be sure to read and work through the next chapter before discussing both chapters as a group.

[My Next Step]

[SEVEN]

GOD AND THE CHARACTER OF JESUS
Look, I Like the Christmas Jesus Best and I'm Saying Grace.

"By being Your Son, yet serving You,
He freed us from servitude
and made us Your sons."
Saint Augustine of Hippo, *Confessions*, X:43

It wasn't uncommon for people to be bewildered when finding out I believed in Jesus in High School. If you grew up in the "Bible Belt," this may not be something you ever had to deal with. Everyone "believes" in God, in some parts of the country, whether they have an authentic faith in Him or not. That's not what it was like growing up in Wyoming. It was much more likely that people would be shocked to find out you believed in God. You were the clear odd man out.

It also wasn't that uncommon for teachers to take shots at the concept of God. This certainly wasn't the first time a teacher had done just this since I began following Jesus in Jr. High, but perhaps it was the most out of the blue. I'm sitting in Freshman English class - at least, I think it was English, it might have been History, either way it wasn't my favorite class to be sure - as the teacher oddly begins talking about a book she loved that outlined the 50 most important people to have ever lived.

The years have not served me well at remembering exactly what led to this moment, but what she said, and the way that she said it still sticks out. I remember her holding the book up for all of us to see. Then, I remember her going straight to number 4 on the list.

"Many of you think Jesus is the most important person in history. Well, according to this..." I think she started giving us the credentials of the author or group that published this book at that point. Either way, it was distinctly odd for her to go straight for the jugular like this. This was a teacher who was rather mild in almost every way.

Unless, that is, you fell asleep in her class. Both times someone managed to fall asleep in class over that semester, this teacher had had a lot of fun with the situation. Once, a kid began nodding off near the front row. The teacher stopped lecturing, went right in front of their desk and made eye contact with them. As their head/body slumped down and then back up again, the teacher squatted and raised to continually make eye contact. She was waiting for the myoclonic jerk reaction to make the situation go her way. She was waiting for that moment where the person's eyes opened suddenly as they drifted a bit too hard and their body reacted so they didn't fall out of the seat.

When it happened, this classmate's eyes locked hard on to the wide-eyes of their teacher just a foot from their face, staring them down. That was rather funny. If I remember it correctly, the other time someone fell asleep it was only a few minutes from the end of class. When the teacher noticed, she again stopped lecturing and asked everyone to leave the room quietly. She wanted this kid to wake up with everyone suddenly gone. That was fun, too.

On this particular day, she was making sure we all caught the fact that this author had only ranked Jesus as the fourth most important person in all of human history. She added an element of pageantry not often seen in her class. There was something about this ranking that she specifically wanted each person in the class to process. I don't remember the topic going anywhere or tying to any specific lesson, I think she just really wanted to revel in that point. Really, if you think about it, considering the billions and billions of people who have lived across known history, number four isn't that bad, really. Actually, it is flat astonishing.

Except no.

It's a nice thought and all, but even if you discard, as this author and the teacher certainly did, that whole dying for the sins of the world and resurrecting from dead, the impact Jesus the Christ has had on this world is far above and beyond that of any other living human being, ever. Of the perhaps eight or nine billion souls to have ever graced this planet, Jesus's is far and away the single most impactful life, even at a paltry 33 years, to have ever landed in the history books. It's not even a contest.

If you were to trace all of the elements of modern society back to their origin point, you find an intricate web that in many cases lead back to the Jewish Messiah. This fact is lost on most today. In his exemplarily work *Who Is This Man?: The Unpredictable Impact of the Inescapable Jesus*, author John Ortberg notes that, "Jesus is history's most familiar figure[18]."

The examples of this truth would simply be too many to list in even a library of books. Here are just a few. Hospitals, prior to corporations turning them into places to drain sick people of their money, find their origin in men who took seriously the parable of Good Samaritan. Just take a drive by the hospitals in your town... or, you know, google them... and see how many have the word "Saint," "Baptist," "Methodist," or other such words in their name.

Orphanages and adoption services trace their inception all the way back to early Christians who decided that the practice of exposure, which means literally leaving a child you didn't want out to die from the elements, was counter to their faith even if it was not their own child. These men of faith began taking in the children of others in order to save these babies' lives. Now-a-days, the government takes on this task, but the origin is rooted in the people of Jesus.

Sunday school, now an outdated relic in most churches, was founded in order to train young men and women who would otherwise be uneducated due to the needs of their family for them to begin working and producing as early in life as possible. Nearly every Ivy League institution finds its origin in the desire to educate people better in the way of Jesus. As Ortberg notes, "...virtually the entire Western system of education and scholarship would arise because of His followers. The insistence on universal literacy would grow out of an understanding that this Jesus, Who was Himself a teacher who highly praised truth, told His followers to enable every person in the world to learn[19]."

Long before the #MeToo movement, it was Jesus' treatment and acceptance of women that began to unravel the common practice of women having no rights and being considered property. Jesus regularly empowered women in His ministry. It was through women that His early work was largely funded. It was also Jesus who chose to first appear to women after His resurrection from the dead, even though in that society the words of a woman were not even permissible as evidence in court.

It isn't just women who find their modern day rights originating in the teaching and work of Jesus, either. The Roman world was historically cruel to the diseased, the malformed, and the handicapped. It was those who took seriously the teachings of Jesus about the "least of these" who changed our entire way of thinking about such individuals. Where in the ancient world the handicapped were pushed out, or even "mercy" killed, it is because of Jesus that even the most broken or different among us is seen as inherently valued.

I could keep listing examples of Jesus's irreducible impact on every aspect of modern society for pages and pages. Ortberg's work has an even more exhaustive list, so I recommend beginning there. However, for just a moment, I'd like to turn our attention to the Bible.

What does the Bible have to do with Jesus? The central character of both the Old and New Testaments of the Bible is ultimately Jesus. The Bible is His story. Like Jesus, the Bible has left an enduring mark on the world. Even popular YouTuber Matthew Santoro, known more for his funny conspiracy theory videos and "50 Amazing Facts" lists the Bible as the most influential book in history, even over every other "holy book[20]."

The chief literary work that has Jesus and His followers handprints all over it is the Bible. Far above any other book, holy book, or literally any other form of writing, the Bible is history's best selling writ by a galaxy-sized landslide. That doesn't count all of the Bibles given for free, or tools like Life.Church's Bible app, which sees millions of free users every day. The Bible is constantly referenced in popular media, even though Hollywood is generally against its truth. The Bible is the source and inspiration for much of the world's greatest artwork and artists of all genres. It is also the most banned book in history, even being made into the chief MacGuffin in other books, such as *Fahrenheit 451*.

There has literally never been another book like it. The Bible is 66 books, written by over 40 different authors (our Catholic branches of the tree have a few more of each), over a span of 1,500 years and yet there is not a single major inconsistency in the message of the text. If you have ever played a game of telephone, where one person whispers a specific message in someone's ear who whispers what they heard and remember in someone else's ear, and so on, you realize just how amazing this is. It is difficult to go fifteen minutes with a very simple message in a room of ten people and still end up with even remotely close to the same message that you started with.

That's not all. There are over 24,000 partial and complete manuscript copies of the New Testament in existence. Some of these can be confidently dated to within just 90 years of their original writings (called "autographs" by scholars). Additionally, there are over 86,000 quotations found in early literature, such as the writings of the early church fathers and lectionaries (church service books containing Scriptural quotes).

Adding to the simply unthinkable veracity of the Bible, there are very few variants found in the text, which would be the switching of words, missing letters, and etc. When comparing our earliest copies with current scholarly translations, in 99% of cases the original text can be reconstructed with practical certainty.

While we consider *Gaelic Wars* a critically important source for much of what we know about ancient Rome, and even Caesar himself, we have just 10 manuscript copies of the work and each of these is separated from the autograph (original writing) by around 1,000 years. Ten copies, compared to over 24,000 copies and over 86,000 direct quotations. We rarely question the authenticity or impact of works by Plato, Homer, and Caesar, which have far far less verifiable authenticity and a much wider gap between our earliest copies and their original writing, and yet we doubt the most tested, challenged, banned, and contested book in all of human history. Do you see how the evidence is beginning to add up?

There has **NEVER** been another book like this in all of human history, holy or common. Similarly, there has **NEVER** been another life like Jesus'. His impact is uncontested. Just the simple fact that we are still talking about Jesus over 2,000 years after His death should tell us something. The fact that up to half of human population still attempts to live by His teachings in some form or fashion adds to the provable depth of His unending impact on all of humanity.

Again, this does not even begin to scratch the surface of the impact that Jesus has had on this world. This also still discounts His physical resurrection, which is perhaps the most attested to and verifiable truth in all of human history. It doesn't take into account that it was Jesus who died on a cross for your sins (and mine), without which we would not have any hope in this life or in the next.

Jesus literally changed everything, everywhere, in every remote corner of the universe, and His impact continues to be felt even in the places that are the most openly hostile to His teachings. As Yale historian Jaroslav Pelikan has written, "Regardless of what anyone may personally think or believe about Him, Jesus of Nazareth has been the dominant figure in the history of Western culture for almost twenty centuries. If it were possible, with some sort of super magnet, to pull up out of history every scrap of metal bearing at least a trace of His name, how much would be left[21]?"

If you doubt the impact of this Middle-Eastern, olive-skinned, unattractive (see Isaiah 53:2), Jewish Messiah and how He and His people have forever changed nearly every aspect of modern life, I encourage you to begin a quest of your own inspecting the data. I have long told those I have taught, whether in my church or through college classes I have led, that if you think there is even a chance that either Jesus or The Bible is false, you should dedicate your entire life to disproving them, for the good of everyone.

This would truly be the noblest quest you could undertake for all of mankind. If, by some sort of anti-miracle, the historical resurrection of Jesus, the veracity of the Holy Bible, or the reality of a loving God is actually false, then every living person needs to know about it. However, if you, like a long line of genius-level intellects before you, cannot disprove these core truths, you will have done something equally as great for yourself.

But, what does this have to do with God?

Who is this God Person, *Anyway*?

As C. S. Lewis famously argued[22], Jesus was never merely a good teacher. Jesus is not merely a good person with some good ideas that moral people should look to for inspiration. Jesus isn't merely a perfect prophet. Jesus wasn't just a holy man. <u>Jesus claimed to be God in the flesh.</u> He didn't mince words about it, either.

Multiple times in His life - again, the most attested to and accounted for life in human history, before Facebook, Twitter, and Instagram had us showing the world every thought we have and every meal we eat - Jesus claimed that He is God. He boldly asserted that there is no other name under heaven by which mankind can be saved, and He is the only way to an eternity in "the good place." Someone who is simply a good moral teacher cannot make those claims. The very extremist nature of the comments exclude him from being either "good" or truly "moral" if He is wrong.

As Lewis posits the argument, He is either a liar, a lunatic, or He is exactly who He says He is. There are literally no other options. Again, should you fall into the category of those believing He was one of the first two, please do everyone still living a favor and commit your life to disproving that Jesus actually was and is the one and only living and true God and only way to heaven.

If, on the other hand, you are or have become at least a little convinced that He is Lord of all, there is still something vastly important that you must come to understand. What I am about to tell you blew my mind in no uncertain terms. Though I should have understood this concept much earlier in my relationship with Jesus, I simply didn't. However, once I came to understand what I am about to tell you, it literally changed everything and every part of me forever.

God is **entirely** consistent with the person of Jesus Christ.

Stay with me here. Jesus claimed He is God. He said that anyone who wants to see the nature and character of the Father need only to look to Him. Hebrews 1:1-3 (CSB) says, "Long ago God spoke to the fathers by the prophets at different times and in different ways. In these last days, He has spoken to us by His Son. God appointed Him heir of all things and made the universe through Him."

Should this be all we know about Jesus, we would have a lifetime of meat to chew on. God created everything through Jesus. He is how God speaks to us in modern life, no longer through prophets and sages who had a special connection to God. Jesus is also the heir of everything God owns, which - *spoiler alert* - Psalm 24:1 says is absolutely every single one of the things.

However, this is far from the most mind-exploding thing this text says. It goes on, "The Son is the radiance of God's glory and the exact representation of His nature, sustaining all things by His powerful Word. After making purification for sins, He sat down at the right hand of the

Majesty on high." Here, again, we see that Jesus is the exact representation of the nature and character of God.

The fullness of this hasn't yet set in. Many people try to "understand" God/god. Many try to dream up what He/She/It might be like "for them." This text proves to us that we don't need to dream up Flying Spaghetti Monsters and imagine what God might just be like. Instead, as one version of Hebrews 1:1-3 gloriously illustrates, Jesus has "translated" Him for us. Jesus is God. Jesus is the EXACT representation of the nature and character of God.

This means that wherever you see Jesus in Scripture or in truthful history, whatever you see Him doing, however you see responding to broken people, whenever you see Him reprimanding religious people... wherever you see Him investing in unexpected people... **WHATEVER you see Jesus doing in Scripture, there you are seeing the EXACT representation of the nature, character, and majesty of God.**

Jesus isn't just some good moral teacher. Jesus isn't simply a prophet. Jesus isn't just a priest of God. He is all of these things, but He claimed to be King of kings and Lord of lords. He is God with human flesh on. According to Hebrews, when and where we see Jesus, we are seeing the living embodiment of the nature and character of God.

Perhaps this is why Matthew 12:21 says that the name of Jesus will be the hope of the world. You see, in the ancient world, the term "name" meant so much more than what your mother yelled when it was time to come in for dinner. The word "name" directly correlated to the expected character of the person whom you were dealing with. This is why in one portion of Scripture a child is renamed from "son of my sorrow" to "son of my right hand." When you said someone's name, you were proclaiming something about that person, you were anticipating the experience of their character.

Jesus is the exact representation of the nature and character of God. His "name" has been proven to be above the angels of heaven. When we see Jesus, we see the character of God. This means that we can understand how God is interacting with us by seeing how Jesus treated people. Take for example, the woman caught in adultery in John 8:1-11.

In this text, we see religious leaders who are trying to prove that Jesus is less than what He claims to be. However, in the midst of this un-winnable scenario (they were literally trying to put him in a Kobiashi-Moru, like in the first of the new *Star Trek* movies) the religious try to trap Jesus in, we also get a clue as to how Jesus responds to us in our sin and failures.

The setting to the scene is that these men have caught a woman in the act of having sexual intercourse in an adulterous manner. The way in which they knew this woman was being adulterous is shadily left out by these religious hypocrites, as is the fact that only the woman is brought before Jesus for justice, not the equally guilty man. In the law of Moses, as they remind the very One who ultimately authored the Law of Moses, such a woman should be stoned to death for her crimes against God.

Jesus doesn't answer them. In fact, Jesus does what perhaps more of us should do and simply ignores these religious hypocrites. At least, this is what He does at first. However, as these "elders" press Jesus more and more, He stands up and simply utters one Kobiashi-Moru breaking statement. "He who is without sin may cast the first stone."

I love what this text says. It notes that each person left. However, it is the manner in which they left that really gets me. They leave from oldest to youngest. The older I get, the more aware of my own shortcomings I am. When I was a kid, I thought I could do no wrong. When I was a teenager, I thought I could do no right. It hasn't been until my mid-thirties, as a father of two and husband for a decade, that I realize just how broken I really am. Yes, broken. After more than a decade and a half of serving in ministry. After a decade of marriage. After having lived for a full three years longer than Jesus. I now realize more than ever in my life just how much I fall short.

These men did, as well. From oldest to youngest they walked away. Perhaps they were waiting for Jesus to throw that stone. As the only person to have ever lived without any sin, He was the one who had the right. He was the one who could have thrown a stone. If he had, it would have been fair game for these religious leaders to pick up their rocks and end this woman's life in the most horrific way imaginable. Think about it, if you were that woman, you would want the first rock to hit you hard in the head, because if they started at your feet, you would experience a series of painful blows that would certainly make you desire death's sweet release.

However, Jesus didn't throw a rock. The religious, old to young, realized how serious He was and how short they fell. Soon, Jesus was alone with this woman. "Does no one condemn you?" He asks her. Notice what He is saying to her, but notice even more what He is saying to us. Jesus doesn't condemn her. She was caught in the very act of unlawful sex and yet Jesus doesn't condemn her.

This is just one small example of how His name is truly the hope of all the world. We rightly should be condemned for our sins and shortcomings. The Bible is clear that these break our relationship with God and make us fall short of Him. Romans 3:23 is crystal clear that this is a universal human problem. We all need to know that God doesn't condemn us if we accept forgiveness for our sins through the sacrificial life of Jesus.

But, He doesn't stop there, either. Had Jesus simply left things at "we're all good," we would have a "the dude abides" sort of Jesus who doesn't line up with the revealed character of God any more than the "god of unquenchable wrath" does. Jesus' next words are powerful, "Neither do I condemn you, **but go and sin no more**." Notice the amazing things we learn about the character of God in this simple interaction. God doesn't condemn those who turn to Him. Our sins are already paid for on a Roman cross. We cannot earn our way to heaven. We cannot earn God's favor. It is finished.

However, that doesn't mean sin is without a price. Jesus didn't let her off the hook and say, "go have fun with your adulterous fling. Hope you both enjoy each other's bodies. After all, all sex is good in the eyes of God and you kids should just live in your truth and enjoy life. That's what's really important." Nope. Not the character of God. Not the heart of Jesus. Jesus tells her to "go and sin no more." In doing so, He proves that God is fully love and God is fully holy. He is not half-full of either.

When we look at how Jesus responds to people in Scripture, we see how God will respond to us in our day-to-day lives, as well. The more we study the Gospel of Jesus, the more we invest our attention to the truth and narrative it contains, the more we uncover the beauty of who God really is. Everywhere we see Jesus, we see the heart of God in action. The more we, like those counterfeit dollar bills mentioned in a previous chapter, examine the real thing in Jesus, the less likely we are to fall for a mischaracterization of God. If something, whether a truth or an idea, is truly of God, it has to line up with the person, work, character, and name of Jesus. If it doesn't, it's not really God.

In this chapter, we've only begun to scratch the smallest layer of the surface of even one small moment in Jesus's life (though it certainly wasn't small to that woman!), and yet we already see some amazing truths about God. The more we understand the life of Jesus, the more the Gospels become a lens for understanding God. However, because the Bible is remarkably consistent from the very first word on the page, when we understand this we also begin to uncover how Jesus is found on every page of the Old Testament, as well. From Genesis to Revelation, Jesus is the subject.

When we realize that Jesus is the exact representation of the nature and character of God and begin reading Scripture through this lens, we begin to discover truly who this God Person really is. As Matthew 12:21 notes, it also gives us hope. When we uncover the reality of "Jesus is God" and all the unending depths that has to offer, we not only find hope in eternity, but discover an invitation to a new way to live life in the present.

We have so much more to unpack about who God is, but the concept presented in this chapter alone is enough for you to go and uncover the most amazing depths about God. Jesus is the **EXACT** representation of the nature and character of God. Without engaging in too much hyperbole...

This changes literally every single one of the things.

[For Personal Growth]

Read Hebrews 1:1-3 at least three times. On your final read through, pause with each phrase and listen for what God is saying to you.

How does it impact your life that Jesus is the exact representation of God's nature and character?

[With A Group]

As a group, read and discuss John 8:1-11.

What surprises you? What challenges you? What are you noticing for the first time? What stands out to you?

How have you seen God as an unrelenting pharaoh in the past?

How does Jesus' life, ministry, and revealed character challenge your view of God?

What else do you know about Jesus that shows you the true nature of God?

As time allows, share and discuss anything from these two chapters that challenged you.

[My Next Step]

[EIGHT]

GOD vs THE VOICES INSIDE MY HEAD

Other Than The Voices In My Head, I Think I'm Pretty Normal.

"The blame is his who chooses: God is blameless."
Plato

Before Amazon.com hit U.S. retailers like a planet-killing asteroid to the dinosaurs, I worked for around seven years at a once hugely popular Big-box store. I had landed this job rather unexpectedly while I was still in High School. My grandmother (I call her Grammy), needed a dishwasher and wanted my help picking one out. We went to this Big-box store, avoiding the "softer side," and going straight for the appliances. Unfortunately, no one was found to help us. Without an official representative of the company to provide answers, I began showing Grammy the different models and explaining the differences in them by simply reading the product description on the sales cards and then adding my thoughts.

Before a sales associate could be found, I had sold my grandmother on a specific model. Little did I know, the store manager had happened upon this part of the sales floor at just the right time and observed what was going on. Not only did we walk out with a dishwasher that night, but I found myself with a job as that company's newest salesman, too.

I stayed with this job for around seven years and across three different states. As I joined the team at one of our Oklahoma City stores, I found myself once again needing to get acquainted with the workers on the sales floor. In this particular Big-box chain, each of us worked as consultive salesmen and saleswomen, earning only commission. This effectively made each of the persons I worked with both my competition and my friends at the same time.

This odd social/economic dynamic was something you had to balance, as you needed to make as many sales as possible to earn a living, and yet would often work with the same shift or rotation of people every day. In this new store, I found myself frequently working with a man named Zsolt (pronounced zhuh-olt... it's just like jolt, but with a buzzing z at the start).

Like me, Zsolt was on the academic track. Unlike me, Zsolt was nearer to becoming a PhD candidate than one seeking a Bachelor's degree. When Zsolt soon found out what it was I was studying to become, our conversations quickly got interesting. Zsolt was an intellectual atheist who loved the thrill of a good debate. He was also much smarter and more quick witted than I was. This meant that the roughly two hours or so of downtime we had with each new shift became grounds for interesting philosophical and theological conversations about God, the Universe, and everything.

While I have never shied away from a constructive, friendly, and lively debate (all of which these conversations held to), it was very apparent to me that Zsolt's intelligence and wit were not something I could conquer on my own. After several weeks of debate and having felt no positive ground was being made on my part, I decided to pull out the big guns. One day, Zsolt mentioned that if there was a book I wanted him to read, he would power through it. This gave me a smile. I knew just the book. I knew just the author. I would meet him like for like.

The next day I brought my worn copy of a book written by an extremely intelligent Oxford professor who had long been an atheist before he sought seriously to disprove the existence of God for himself. This book had actually been a series of radio spots and lectures given across the second Word War, which were later compiled and edited into a book called *Mere Christianity*. In this work, C. S. Lewis presents some of the most intelligent argumentation for the existence and reality of a personal God that I had ever read. Much of what he wrote was over my own head, so I figured it would hit Zsolt right where he lived.

The next day, Zsolt returned the book to me, claiming to have read through the entire thing. I had my doubts. There was almost no way he had read, let alone fully comprehended what Lewis had to say in a single sitting. Then again, he was much smarter than me. This landed on me as a stunning blow. I wasn't ready for Zsolt. I had expected that we would dive into a discussion on the universal moral law that Lewis presents, but instead, Zsolt didn't even engage me about that work at all. He simply made some comments about faulty logic and moved on.

In hindsight, I should have pressed him. Perhaps he had read it... but, his avoidance certainly should have meant that he didn't really process through it. Instead of pressing, I let things go and put my intellectual dukes down for just long enough for Zsolt to move into his next round of blows.

"Did you know that Hitler was a Christian, and that the holocaust was caused because he read the Bible?"

I didn't want to look stupid, but I had never heard this argument before. Hitler a Christian? Could that be? In that moment, I was set back on my heels. I suddenly felt the weight of needing to know a lot more about one of the most horrific and important, for very wrong reasons, moments in human history. My mind raced. I couldn't think.

I had come prepared to discuss Lewis' well thought out arguments in *Mere Christianity*. I had not come prepared to defend Jesus's reputation against Hitler, of all people. Of course, since Lewis was an Englishman writing in the time of the Second Great War, perhaps I should have had at least a little foresight to see this all coming. Rather than stay on track with our planned discussion of Lewis' masterpiece, I was completely caught off guard and couldn't come up with a coherent answer. I was tied up in a knot. Zsolt smiled. He had taken this round from me without even throwing a single punch.

That next day I went to one of my professors with a heavy mind and a confused heart. Maybe that should be the other way around? I needed to know how to counter this Hitler thing. I needed to know the exact words and phrases that would help me win this argument. I couldn't return again as the one-legged man in the butt-kicking contest where everyone else but me was wearing pointy boots and spurs. I just couldn't.

I just knew this specific professor would have exactly the right answers. I went to him in that moment like the rebel alliance had gone to Obi-Wan. He was my only hope. As I began to explain the first phase of the multi-part quandary I was going through, my professor quickly cut me off.

"It's a red herring," he said.

"What?" I stammered. I was having a really hard time understanding what fish had to do with anything in this moment.

"It's a red herring. He is using a logical fallacy against you," the professor said, before noticing my obvious confusion and adding, "He is throwing you off track so he doesn't even need to win the argument. He's simply letting you beat yourself."

"So I don't need to research if Hitler was a Christian?" I responded.

He simply gave me a look, tilted his head, scrunched up his lips and eyebrows, and said, "Come on. You're smarter than that."

While I had wished in that moment that those words were true, I knew that my professor was right. As I looked back, I had gotten off track in almost every argument. No matter what great evidence I produced for the existence of God, Zsolt didn't counter my sound logic, he simply moved things off point and into unfamiliar and unexpected territory. He was keeping me soundly in his court. I was hooking every red herring that he placed in the water for me. I was devouring that fish whole.

As soundly as my defeat was handed to me, there was something else wrong with this. I wasn't allowing myself to be led by the Holy Spirit. I wasn't as interested in winning Zsolt's eternal soul as I was beating an intellectual Goliath at a battle of wits that I could never have won on my own. I wasn't engaging with the Spirit of God, I was being beaten in the battlefield of the mind.

Unfortunately, this story isn't just my own. It is highly likely in your journey towards God that you have been engaged in a battle of wits with an enemy (Zsolt wasn't my enemy, just to be clear) who has a habit of diverting your attention and getting you off track. Each of us has an enemy in this world.

The Bible consistently refers to this fallen one as **our** enemy, not God's. It is not as if there are co-eternal and co-equal forces, one good and one bad. God is the only preexistent being. Everything else was created by Him. While everything was created good, we humans and angels alike were given a capacity for free will. We were given the ability to choose God or to choose against God. Somewhere in the distant reaches of the ancient past, satan fell from heaven like lightning because he desired to be God.

This fallen one, often called "the devil," has been on a quest to steal, kill, and destroy ever since. As a part of this quest, the devil has a habit of taking the good functions of our mind/spirit/body that God gave us for good and tricking us into doing the enemy's handiwork. This is where our discussion of another popular misconception of God must begin.

You see, many people confuse the action of God in their lives with that spider-sense He put into us that we call our conscience. The word conscience literally means "with knowledge." It is that pinprick of insight and knowledge you feel when you perceive that something you've just done, or are considering doing, is not right.

However, it is important that we examine how the enemy can use our conscience against us if we are truly to understand what we believe about God in a very practical sense. After all, trust and commitment are the result of knowledge. The more we get to know God and experience Him, the better we come to trust Him and give our lives to Him. As Mike Bickle has said, "You will never be more committed to God than you know He is committed to you."

So, how can our consciences impact our view of God? J. B. Phillips has noted in his fantastic (and ironically rather diminutive in size) work *Your God Is Too Small* that, "to many people conscience is almost all they have by way of knowledge of God. This still small voice which makes them feel guilty and unhappy before, during, or after wrong-doing, is God speaking to them... Yet, to make conscience into God is a highly dangerous thing to do[23]." In other words, like Zsolt turned my own arguments against me, the devil often turns our own conscience against us.

What we rarely come to understand when it comes to the God-given gift of our natural conscience is that it can easily become malformed and broken. We have the ability, which is amplified over time, to condition our conscience to become too sensitive or too hardened. On the one hand, a person can abuse their conscience to the point where they mourn over every bug they maybe even might have accidentally stepped on. On the other hand, a person can atrophy their conscience to a point where even mass murder barely makes them batt a guilty eyelid.

If, as Phillips suggests, many people have come to confuse the function of their conscience with the action of God, the God they will come to believe in will become warped and twisted as well. Sin has the power in our lives, should we let it, to scar our conscience and beat it into tough leather. Sin, accompanied by a hyperactive sense of guilt, can also cause us to seek harsh penance for even the smallest slight against our self-made god. On the one hand, our consciences can become too sensitive. On the other hand, our consciences can nearly cease to function at all.

Allow me to use Oklahoma's propensity for tornadoes as an example once more. Back when I first moved to OKC, as I mentioned in a previous chapter, I was so nervous when tornado season hit that I would have spent a lot of time taking shelter were it not for my Okie-native roommate. Fast forward to our final tornado season in Oklahoma, however, and you would see a very different picture.

In our final tornado season, only the second one we experienced with our young son, and just a year after that massive tornado had eaten our city like it was Pac-man gobbling up pixelated dots, we found ourselves in a moment where the skies around us had predictably darkened. Winds began to howl through the thin walls of our starter home in a very telling manner. We should have been panicked. Yet, neither my wife nor I took much notice at all.

We had been through this exercise so much in the past several years that our wills, emotions, and perhaps even our consciences had been deadened to the imminent threat of death all around us that came with each tornado season. Even as the sirens began going off, my wife and I casually continued our conversation, glancing only occasionally towards the 4Warn storm team on our TV.

If this moment of our lives had been a horror movie, people would be screaming at their screens for us to get out of that house. They would have been begging us to go and get our son and get to shelter. The reality was, however, we had been dulled to the weight of that threat. Even though the news, the rain, and the sirens were all warning us that something was coming, we had allowed ourselves to become hardened to this situation.

It is important to note that we were making our preparations as we were talking in that moment. It is also important to note that we did, though perhaps a little too casually, make our way over to our neighbor's storm shelter with at least a minute or two to spare before the hail started hammering the world around us like the last remaining member of an enemy paintball team. It just didn't seem to phase us any longer.

Think about that. As I describe this scenario, you may feel a little tense inside. You may wonder how we could have ever gotten to a point where we would so casually traipse through such a life-threatening situation. And, you'd be right. But, I bet you also have become numb to certain things in your own life, as well. Perhaps when you first moved to your city your heart went out to the beggar who was at that one particular street corner. Now, however, you can't remember the last time you even realized that he or she was still there.

For a certain generation, I would wager that the first time you saw partial nudity on prime-time TV, you thought about writing a letter to the editor and never again watching that particular show, or even boycotting the network entirely. Now, however, you barely even notice the soft-core porn streaming services serve up with each and every new show on their packed slate. It is all too easy to become numb to things with exposure.

What else in your life did you once notice immediately, and yet now you couldn't even be bothered to see if you tried? "Conscience can be so easily perverted or morbidly developed in the sensitive person, and so easily ignored and silenced in the insensitive, that it makes a very unsatisfactory god[24]."

Perhaps someone you've known has been on the edge of sanity because of something they had done that most would consider a minor deal. Because they had trained their conscience to attack them for every little offense, they became a nervous wreck. Perhaps, on the other hand, someone you've known has so callously damaged someone or something, and then felt little to no remorse after. Both are examples of a malformed conscience.

When we try to make the function of our conscience into the action of God, we end up with a god who is either too extremely harsh or so completely passive. In either case, we do not have the one true God as described in the Bible. So, if God cannot be limited to or contained within the function of our conscience, then who is this God Person, anyway? We will get to that in a moment, but first...

It wasn't until many years later that I learned the true irony of Zsolt's question. Was Hitler really a Christian? I would most confidently say not. Did Hitler really follow the Bible? "You shall know them by their fruit." Did Hitler understand how to warp a nation's collective conscience so that he could bend an entire people to his will? Absolutely.

As Phillips notes, "In Nazi Germany, of course, propaganda as a weapon to pervert the moral sense became a fine art. It soon seemed, for example, a positive duty to hate the Jews, and a good Nazi would doubtless have suffered pangs of conscience if he had been kind to one of the despised race[25]."

To paraphrase Phillips' conclusion, these examples show how dangerous it can be to confuse that voice inside our head with God. "Obviously, this invaluable moral sense can be rightly trained and even rightly influenced... provided we can be sure what we mean by right. But to define that word we need to discover God[26]."

[For Personal Growth]

Read Colossians chapter 2. Write down and examine anywhere the text reveals something about our fallen nature or God's perfect nature.

How does the fall of man in Genesis 3 reshape our conscience and will?

If you were honest, would you say that your conscience is too sensitive, too dull, or functioning as God intended?

Why do you say this?

[With A Group]

Continue reading the next chapter before discussing both chapters as a group.

[My Next Step]

[NINE]

GOD AS HOLY SPIRIT
Goin' Up to the Spirit in the Sky.

"We are not all we were made to be when everything in our
lives and churches can be explained apart from
the work and presence of the Spirit of God."
Francis Chan, *Forgotten God*, 18

While I was very loyal to my church as a teen, there was a short season where I also attended another church. The reason I began attending this other church, of course, was a girl. A beautiful girl named Jana caught my eye and I wanted to spend more time with her, plain and simple.

It didn't take long for me to realize that this other church was… different from what I was used to. This particular branch of the Christian tree was what some would simply call "charismatic," however it would later prove that even that word was not quite suitable enough. I first noticed a difference when the pastor's daughter and her boyfriend very noticeably broke up during one youth meeting. What started as a normal night soon descended into a shouting match between the two, right in the church lobby.

In fairness to the now-ex boyfriend, this girl was poking the bear big time. Whatever he had done to anger her, she was taking every jab at him she could get in. However, this didn't excuse the words that loudly came out of his mouth in front of everyone.

"I'm going to kill you for this."

I think everyone in the area paused. All of our eyes got really wide as all of our mouths shut really tight. It was a "moment," for sure. I didn't really know this girl, who just happened to be the pastor's daughter, but what she revealed next helped me learn new things about her.

"Do it. My dad will just resurrect me. He is in touch with God, he can do it." I don't remember the exact words that surrounded the key thought, but "My dad will resurrect me," stood out and I do remember hearing exactly that. Those aren't words you tend to forget, especially when someone is saying them with such boldness and confidence.

It would be easy to chalk this up to the hormonal words of a teenager who was in the midst of a break-up, but there was just something so matter of fact about the whole encounter. I can't say for sure, but it seemed as if she really believed this. Had this been an isolated incident, I might not even remember this strange moment. However, it was not. It was VERY not.

Sometime later I attended my first and only service of the main church, not just the youth program. What I experienced there helped me to understand where this pastor's daughter's confusing words found their source. Perhaps what I am about to describe is somewhat normal for you. I apologize if I make it seem strange in anyway. It was strange for me.

The pastor preached a very fiery sermon with lots of sweat and spit thrown in to lubricate the words he claimed God had for us. I was used to a very intellectual presentation of the Gospel with deep life application. What I experienced here was very much like that shouting match this man's daughter had had with her now ex-boyfriend. Except in this case it was the pastor vs seemingly every other person in the room, and he was intent upon winning the fight.

I don't remember what this man preached on. I do remember vividly what happened as a part of the closing to his sermon. I was sitting near the front. At least, I was near enough to see what was happening very well.

This man called people up to the front. Perhaps he invited them and they chose to come up? Either way, people were standing in front of the stage/pulpit area in a wide row. This pastor would come up to them with a white hanky in hand, and he would speak something loudly and in a very preacher-y way of speaking. I don't think I knew how to describe it other than "preacher-y." It was a special language that I had only accidentally happened across on a TV channel once.

After speaking over each person, one at a time, the pastor would lay his open palm on their forehead and with his entire body would push forward suddenly. Inevitably, each person would fall backward onto the floor, still and quiet. As the pastor's arm pushed forward and after the person's body would begin to fall, his arm and hand would shake. Meanwhile, the person whom he had just pushed would lay there, seemingly until everyone had had their turn.

I grew up watching professional wrestling, so this was a move I had only ever before seen on WWF (as it was called back then) television. It was quite the finishing move. My eyes were wide. I didn't know what to make of this experience. I seem to remember turning to someone from the youth group who was near me and asking what was going on. They explained to me that he was slaying them in the Spirit. I still didn't quite get it. I kept looking at what was happening and then looking back at this person.

"What if the Spirit isn't really moving in them when he pushes on their head?" I seem to remember asking.

"Oh sometimes people just fall over anyway so they don't cause a scene," I believe the person responded. I couldn't bring myself to come back after that.

Fast forward a few years. In another somewhat random occurrence I found myself in another charismatic church in the south for a big special gathering. On this particular night several people spoke. Nearly every one of them broke into the speaking of tongues. Especially the main speaker. He would be sharing the message God had for that church that night and then suddenly in the middle of a sentence would be speaking something that sounded like "Ah Shada da da da" followed by some other words... Whatever the words were, I heard them enough and from a variety of people from the stage that night that, while I still don't know what was said, I do know some of them were saying the same thing over and over again.

As the night went on, multiple people began speaking in tongues and often all at the same time. It might have sounded like a chorus, except that each was speaking louder and louder so that no one person could clearly be heard, and while the "ah shada da da da" was likely there in the mix, it did distinctly sound like a cacophony.

People were also dancing. Nothing against dancing, but this wasn't any sort of dancing I had ever seen. When I asked someone what was going on, they replied that people were being slain in the Spirit. There was the phrase again.

Still, something about the whole night felt off in my own spirit. I asked a trusted pastor friend about this and he walked me through what Scripture commands in terms of speaking in tongues and orderly worship. The more we looked at those verses, the less I could confidently say that was what I had experienced. He also jokingly gave me a little heads up "in case I was in that sort of a situation again and need to fake speaking in tongues."

I told him I was pretty sure I shouldn't fake something like that, but that he should go on and tell me.

"One phrase. You only need one phrase. Say it after me, 'She came in a Honda. She left in a Suzuki.'"

"What?"

"Say it, 'She came in a Honda. She left in a Suzuki.'"

I said that. He encouraged me to say it again, only faster. Each time I said it, he had me say it again, only a little faster and with a little different emphasis.

"She came in a Honda. She left in a Suzuki. She came in a Honda. She left in a Suzuki."

"There you go." He said. "Just say that over and over, fast and with some twang to your voice and you're all set."

I laughed.

Fast forward one last time. I am working as a youth pastor and we are in Joplin, Missouri, helping the city recover from a deadly F5 tornado. As it would turn out, we ended up helping in much the same way that we would end up serving in our own city of Moore, Oklahoma a year or two later. We were staying at a host church in Joplin that served as "home base" for mobilizing volunteers who would come in for one week at a time.

Come Wednesday night, the space where we would typically relax and hang out at the end of a long day of tearing down homes and getting them ready for bulk cleanup became this church's youth gathering space once more. As it became time for a response after his message, the youth pastor opened up the altars for people to pray. I just happened to notice that one of the girls who came with us was approached by a member of the host church. For a few minutes this woman was talking to our girl with large gestures and animated movements. Then, the woman pulled our girl in for a long hug.

Not long after, as we were gathering back together in our group, I asked this girl what was happening with the woman who came up and talked her ear off.

"Oh, she said that God had a message for me that I needed to hear and that she was supposed to be the one to tell me."

"Yeah?" I said, as I lifted an eyebrow of suspicion.

"Yeah. She said God told her to tell me that my little sister is going to die this year, but not to worry because He will make me stronger for it."

The way she said those words didn't come from a place of panic. The way she said them was almost dismissive, but not in a worried sort of way that betrayed a sense of doubt. Her tone was filled with more of an annoyed rejection of the words than anything.

"Do you have a sister?" I asked, as this girl was relatively new to our youth group.

"Yep." She said, again without a hint of fear or worry.

"Is she sick or anything like that?"

83

At this point, she laughed. "No. But, don't worry," she added, "that lady was just crazy."

From that point on, "Hey, how's your sister doing?" became my standard greeting with this youth girl. I should point out that her sister didn't die that year. That's probably an important detail. Otherwise, this story would be a little morbid. I'm pretty sure she didn't die that next year either. I think I would remember that. This story would have a very different tone if she had.

Why is it that when we talk about the movement of the Spirit of God in modern society that these sort of stories are all too common? As you look through the pages of Scripture, the Bible and Jesus Himself speak deeply and regularly about the Spirit of God. Scripture records mountains of evidence that God's Spirit indeed moves among us. Yet, many people recoil when you talk about "movements of the Spirit" because they have historically been so misused, misunderstood, and mispronounced among us.

Who Is This God Person, Anyway?

When Francis Chan, author of the bestselling book *Crazy Love*, sat down to write a book about the Holy Spirit, he astutely titled the book *Forgotten God*. In this work, Chan reflects that "whole denominations have been built around specific beliefs about the Holy Spirit. I know people who have lost jobs at churches and Christian colleges because of their beliefs about the Holy Spirit... It is not one of those issues that is easy to float over. This is especially true if you belong to a particular 'camp' with a specific belief or bent[27]."

While most people have no problems referring to God and/or Jesus, when it comes to the Holy Spirit things often get really mucky really quickly. It seems that many of us don't know how to deal with the Spirit, so we either get really weird or really silent. Yet, Scripture talks a lot about the Spirit of God. In fact, Jesus, Himself, said that it was better that He went away so that the Spirit could come upon us!

Many of us avoid the spiritual side of Christianity. It makes us uncomfortable. Let's be honest, when it comes to the Spirit, we either think of ghosts and goblins, or we picture "the force" from Star Wars. We are much more comfortable with an impersonal and uncaring force that runs through all living things and can be manipulated if we just know the right moves, words, or hand gestures than we are a life-giving Spirit Who is co-eternal with the other Members of the Trinity.

As Chan points, out, however, this is not representative of the Spirit of God. The Holy Spirit is not an "it," the Holy Spirit shares the same aspects of personhood that we understand from the Father and the Son. "The Holy Spirit is a Person who has personal relationships with not only believers, as we have seen, but also with the Father and the Son[28]."

Just as God is consistent with the revelation of Father and with the character of Jesus Christ, so too God is Holy Spirit. Historically, the understanding of God as Father, Son, and Holy Spirit has been called the Godhead or the Trinity. While you will not find this theological term in the Bible, these terms do refer to a very Biblical reality.

While scholars often argue that the book of Job may have been the earliest oral or written history of what we now call the Holy Bible, it is the book of Genesis that peers back all the way to the beginning of mankind's earthly history. In Genesis 1:26, God says "Let us make man in our image, according to our likeness" (CSB).

For several years I have led what many churches call a "newcomer's class" or welcoming conversation to provide people who are getting connected with the church a way to explore what we are all about. In each experience I begin the conversation by having our guests read this passage and note what stands out to them.

Invariably, someone will quickly notice for the first time that from page one of the Bible, God self-references in the plural. This always begins an interesting conversation. While most people have off-handedly heard of God as "Father, Son, and Holy Spirit," we still often think of God in the singular. That is also very true.

Without confusing things too much, that God is one is also a thoroughly Biblical understanding. Perhaps the most important statement made in the Jewish history of the Old Testament is, "Listen Israel, the Lord our God: the Lord is One" (CSB). So, how can God be three and yet be One?

Many have attempted to explain this paradigm away in words that our minds can wrap themselves around. I have heard the triunity of God explained by looking at an egg. An egg is a shell, a white substance, and a yolk. Yet, we don't say eggs when we hold just one, we reference it as one single egg. But, the Godhead cannot be so simply defined.

I have also heard the illustration of H_2O. When heated, H_2O presents as steam, in a temperate environment, H_2O presents as water, and at frigid temperatures, H_2O presents as ice. The molecules that make up H_2O do not change, only how they are presented to us. This too helps us wrap our minds around the triunity of God, but also falls short.

I have heard the concept of the Trinity explained by taking a look at man. One man may be a father to his child, a husband to his wife, and a son to his own father. Or, likewise, I have heard the example of how each single human is mind/emotion, body, and soul/spirit. These images may be helpful, but still fall short.

None of these completes a full picture of God, who is one essence, yet still three. Truly, the concept of the Trinity containing the oneness of God becomes a mind-boggling concept the more you digest it. It would be easier to ignore it all together, were it not so completely Biblical. Take, for example, Matthew chapter three's account of the baptism of Jesus.

Jesus, Who is being baptized by John, enters the water. In that moment, the Holy Spirit is descending like a dove on Jesus. Also, God the Father speaks from heaven and says, "this is my beloved Son, with Whom I am well pleased" (Matthew 3:17 CSB). In one pregnant minute in history we see the Trinity interacting together in the same moment of time.

This verse shatters the concept of modalism; that God is three, but not all at once. God is co-existing and eternal. The Father, Son, and Holy Spirit are all accounted for as co-equal, co-eternal, and all completely God. All of this is perfectly summed up in one sentence in Genesis, "Let us create man in our image" (Genesis 1:26, Emphasis added).

No matter how beyond explanation the concept of a Three-in-One Trinitarian Godhead is, the Bible does not allow for any lesser concept. But, once we move beyond the shock that God is singularly plural, there is still something even more mind-bending to look at. God was never alone. God has always existed in a loving relational community.

It is often in this moment of the conversation that I will ask a follow up question; "Why did God create mankind?" Inevitably, the answers I get will include something like, "because God needed something to relate to," or "because God was lonely." In this scenario, mankind is the solution to the problem God had. God was lonely, lacking, and insufficient, so God created mankind to fill a hole and to solve the problem.

This is simply not the case. God has always existed in life-giving community. Before mankind was formed from the dust of the ground and the breath of God (another word for Spirit in Scripture), God existed in a perfect loving community within Himself. God did not lack anything when He created man. God created man because of an overflow of love that God desired to share with His creation. Mankind wasn't created out of *lack*, but out of overflowing, unreasonable, uncontainable *love*.

I say this to correct a very behind the scenes false assumption about God. For some reason we humans get grandiose ideas that God needed us. God needed worship. God needed companionship. God was lacking something. The truth is quite the opposite, God was full to overflowing and created mankind out of an indescribable abundance. We were not created to fill something missing in God, we were created in love by love and through a perfect love in order to experience God's love.

What does this have to do with the Holy Spirit? Frankly, because the Spirit is less "concrete," and is often seen as a mystery, we relegate the Spirit of God to some B-team level team member. We can grasp a historical Jesus. We can wrap our minds around the concept of a Creator and/or Father-figure. When we speak of the Spirit, we immediately move into a mystical plane of existence lacking a physical image.

Perhaps this is why our forefathers referred to this member of the Trinity as the "Holy Ghost." We could not think of a way to personify the Holy Spirit, so we attached the image of a Halloween ghoul to give ourselves a physical representation. As Matthew B. Simms has noted, "Exploring Who God is and how He acts is never-ending. He is more expansive and deep than the universe. As soon as we find out one truth about Who He is, we are amazed as we focus our telescope on that truth that there are a trillion galaxies of truth within that single truth. God is infinite in Who He is[29]."

One such truth that contains a trillion galaxies of truth within is the reality that God is Holy Spirit. In John 14:15-17 and 16:7, Jesus promises His disciples both then and now that the "Comforter" and/or "Counselor" will come upon those who call upon His name when He leaves. The word that Jesus used, which we have translated to "comforter" is Paraclete. Literally, this word means "One who is called alongside to help." The Holy Spirit is our helper! Far from being a mystical force that bends to our command should we know the magic words, the Paraclete is God's Spirit who advocates for us.

It is amazing that we see the Spirit as such a mystery when Scripture speaks deeply to this Member of the Trinity. Just take a look at the truth that Scripture reveals:

The Holy Spirit is the one who convicts us of sin (John 16:8-11).

The Holy Spirit is the agent of change in our lives (Philippians 2:13, Acts 15:8-9).

The Holy Spirit is the Member of the Godhead that dwells in us (Romans 8:9).

The Holy Spirit is our teacher and reveals spiritual truth (John 14:26, John 16:13, 1 Corinthians 2:14).

The Holy Spirit guides us as we witness to others (Luke 12:11-12).

The Holy Spirit is our advocate in prayer, even translating the groaning of our heart that is too deep for words to express (Romans 8:26-27, 1 John 2:1).

The Holy Spirit gives us the power to live victorious lives (Acts 1:8).

The Holy Spirit has a role in purifying our hearts (Acts 15:8-9).

This is just the beginning of what Scripture says of the Spirit. Still, even if you were to read all of the above and look up every single reference, there is still truth to the concept that "the Spirit moves in mysterious ways." The Apostle Paul captures this beauty in his eloquent letter to the Romans:

"In the same way the Spirit also helps us in our weakness, because we do not know what to pray for as we should, but the Spirit Himself intercedes for us with unspoken groaning. And He who searches our hearts knows the minds of the Spirit, because He intercedes for the saints according to the will of God" (Romans 8:26-27 CSB).

What is it that is most beautiful about the mystery created by the triunity of God and the manifestation of the Holy Spirit? God promises us that through the Spirit He will help us. He will intercede for us. He listens to our hearts when we can't even put things into words. One of the beautiful things about the Spirit of God is that God proves Himself as being **for** us. He desires us to know Him better. Just as He did at our creation, God is in perfect loving relationship with Himself to the point of overflowing and He desires that we share in that beauty with Him. The Holy Spirit is - as a part of His interaction with humanity - our conduit to experience that overflow of overwhelming, incomprehensible, and utterly incomparable love.

In our fallen nature, none of us know how to accept this, but God reveals Himself to us through His Spirit. He is here to help. Even when we don't have the right words. Even when we don't know to do anything more than grunt like cave-people discovering fire for the first time in our inner being... God translates our hearts to reveal the heart of God.

Does God heal? Does God allow prophecy? Does God give us words that our tongues have never spoken before? Certainly. Scripture is full of each of these. But, unlike what I had experienced with a few pastors or churches in the past, these "gifts of the Spirit" are not the point.

The Spirit helps us, not to become more full of ourselves or to give us magic powers. The Spirit helps us experience a deeper relationship with God. Anything lesser than that is missing the bullseye.

[For Personal Growth]

Go back and read each of the verses associated with the Spirit of God on page 108.

How does the Holy Spirit, as revealed in Scripture, differ from what you have been taught in the past?

[With A Group]

Go around the group and share a time when you were a kid where your conscience was either too harsh or too lax?

As a group, take turns reading each of the verses referenced on page 108 and discuss each one as you encounter it.

What surprises you? What challenges you? What are you noticing for the first time? What stands out to you?

How does this understanding of the Holy Spirit challenge your existing view of God?

How do you or do you not feel the Spirit moving in your own life?

If there is time, share and discuss anything else from this chapter that challenged you.

Before you close in prayer, have each person share with the group what measurable and practical way you are going to respond to God this week.

[My Next Step]

[TEN]

GOD vs THE EMPIRE OF ROBOTIC SHEEP
So... DO Robots Dream of Electric Sheep?

> "We all went astray like sheep; we all have turned
> to our own way; and the Lord punished
> Him for the iniquity of us all."
> **Isaiah 53:6**

Sometimes I can be a huge jerk, but I have my reasons, at least. Especially when my team is competing in an important game. It's not like I'm alone, either. Lots of people have their home team. It's common to cheer your team on and also silently hope the entire opposing team come down with a very fixable case of malaria the night before the big game. I'm not the only one who does this, I assure you.

It's just that my team isn't a sports-ball team. While some would argue this proves something is broken inside of me, I have no interest whatsoever for organized sports. I don't like watching them on TV. I don't like going to them live. I don't even much like playing them. It's not like I haven't tried. I come from a family of sports-ball watching people. Yet, while they were raving over the latest in-season sport, I spent my time watching professional wrestling. Hulk Hogan was my team and there was no off-season. Well, except for that time that a massive mountain of a man named Earthquake sat on his chest and he had to leave to recover... and/or make another really cheesy movie. "Dooo-kie," indeed.

Perhaps, that tells you all you need to know about me. I appreciate you reading this far. It was a good run. I understand your departure. But, if you're willing to stay with me just a little longer, I promise I am getting to a relatively salient point in a page or two. In the meantime, I need to explain that I have come to understand that whether you're a sports-ball person or not, everyone has their home team of choice.

It just took me a while to figure out the correlation for myself. Back in the 00's, I worked as a Senior Accounts Manager for Dell Computers. While working for Dell, I bought my first iPhone. That was my gateway drug. Sometime later, my wife decided she wanted Apple's newest product, the then newly announced iPad. I was not convinced. "They are just giant iPhones," I lovingly told her. "You don't need a giant iPhone." Ironically, I was the one between the two of us who quickly jumped on the "plus" models of the iPhone when it was released years later.

Soon enough, my wife got her shiny Gen 1 iPad. I was surprised at how quickly I became jealous of this "just a giant iPhone" and how often I tried to steal this from her before I got my own. This process of conversion came to its logical conclusion when I got my first MacBook Pro. The point should not be lost that this was a massive transition for me. Before this purchase, I had spent years selling PC's with a multi-million dollar monthly quota, so I had sold tens of millions of dollars worth of Windows-based product in my corporate career.

I had owned some of Apple's computers before, but this was back in the early 90's before the multi-colored iMac was even a dream. This was back when Steve Jobs had been kicked out of Apple and was working on the first *Toy Story* film. This was back when Windows was king of the hill and Macs were clearly the niche market. Back then, I was literally made fun of for owning "that fruit company's inferior computers."

All of that changed once the iPhone was announced. Suddenly, Apple had the single hottest computing device on the planet. Where Apple was once derided as that small fruit company that shouldn't even pretend to make computers, suddenly the iPhone alone was out-earning everything Microsoft made combined.

With this rise to power also came a change in perception. Suddenly, Apple was the dominant force. Predictably, where Microsoft was once called "big evil," now Apple became the target of people's ire. The very company that changed everything with their "Big Brother" Super Bowl ad, was suddenly the top contender in people's minds for becoming that Orwellian nightmare themselves with each new product launch.

As Apple got bigger and bigger, their detractors got louder and louder. Eventually, those once-brave souls who were seen as the rebels and the "crazy ones," the people who thought different and challenged what people considered to be a computer in the first place... suddenly those rebels had lived long enough to become the empire. Luke had officially become Vader and now a new rebellion rose up. This rebellion, however, was against Apple.

Just as predictably, every technology company on the planet clamored to produce their own "iPhone killer." Many tried. Many died trying. With each new swing and miss, companies proved over and over that Steve Jobs was correct when he noted that the iPhone was 5 years ahead of the competition. However, 5 years isn't really that long of a time and, eventually, the competition caught up. When they did, the "I'm a Mac and I'm a PC" era was replaced by the iOS vs Android super battle.

It was in the heat of this brand struggle that I realized something quite profound. Even though I don't care for sports, all of us have a "home team" that they root for. Some people get up early in freezing temperatures to get to a ball game and tailgate. Others stand in line waiting for each year's iPhone release.

What I came to realize was that my home team wasn't the Denver Broncos. My home team wasn't the Buckeyes. My home team wasn't the Sooners. My home team was Apple, and in much the same way that riotous fanatics can watch the ball game and scream for their team to win and the other team to fail, I was rooting for Apple and hoping with each new encounter that whoever was going up against them would fall flat on their faces.

When Samsung became the latest and greatest pretender to the throne and started taking shots at Apple, that was my Super Bowl. Except, instead of 50-yard lines and passes, it was court room litigation over copyrights and the heated back and forth of dueling product releases. With every commercial Samsung released taking shots at Apple, I, like any good sports-ball fanatic, suddenly hoped that their warehouses burned to the ground, their executive team were tried for treason, and their shareholders all saw negative returns. You know, the normal things sports-ball enthusiasts hope for against the rival team.

During one of these "big game moments," I was at an airport as they announced that if anyone was caught with the particular Samsung phone model that was notoriously catching on fire across the country at the time of boarding a plane, these persons were now committing a <u>federal</u> crime. That's right. If they had the other team's phone and boarded a heavy metal tube that flies through the air, they were going to jail. I cheered out loud as they made that announcement. I'm not kidding at all.

My wife was dreadfully embarrassed and tried to hush me. I had made a scene, yes, but I wasn't crazy. My team was simply ahead $100 Billon to 0 in that moment in the game and I was overcome with excitement that just had to escape my mouth-hole and which rippled outwardly into my extremities causing them to raise into the air.

Just as all rival teams have a bit of back and forth and friendly jesting in their sparring, those who prefer one of the rival teams to my Apple home team came up with a nice little moniker for people like me. We're called "sheeple." As the argument goes, while Apple was once the one telling everyone to "think different," now anyone who is caught buying the latest Apple gadget is nothing more than a mindless sheep, feasting excitedly on every morsel of news and new product that Apple lets "infamously leak" out at predictable intervals.

I must admit, as I sit here writing this on my MacBook Pro, feeling the band to my Apple Watch gently caress the keyboard, as my iPhone rests safely in my pocket, as my iPad Pro sits charging on my desk, and as I watch reruns of Friends on my Apple TV streaming device, "sheeple" might have just the slightest ring of truth to it. Still, the term does sting a little.

A few years ago, a new team was found on the horizon. I think this one may just be the real Super Bowl showdown, too. While other companies tried (*cough* and failed *cough*) to meet Apple head on, this company was determined to beat them at their own game. They didn't copy where Apple was going, they looked ahead and beat everyone to the punch.

Their product? A sentient toilet paper tube that responds when you talk to it. At least, that's what I thought in my head when it was announced, much the same way I derided the "giant iPhone." Where everyone else attempted to play the same game Apple was playing and beat them,

Amazon did something even smarter. They did the very thing Apple had done to Microsoft years prior; they changed the game itself, making everyone else scramble to learn the new rules.

Ironically, this very product, essentially a functional use for Artificial Intelligence, was a key player in *The Hitchhiker's Guide to the Galaxy*. In that book, we find Marvin the depressed robot. Marvin represented the height of everything mankind is seeking to create, a sentient life-form to replace us. However, unlike the days of *The Jetsons*, where chipper Rosey the Robot always had a digital smile, Marvin represented something else entirely. Marvin was mankind's greatest achievement and greatest letdown all at once.

Finally, mankind had created a new form of life, only to discover that it was just as sad and depressed the rest of us. You see, for a long time Science Fiction had this fantasy of man creating robots who would take all of the aspects of life we didn't want to deal with and happily get the task done. Eventually, Sci-Fi became reality, and so, we created robot vacuums. We created always-connected appliances. We created Alexa, Siri, and their contemporaries.

But, what happens next? What is the logical direction of this great technological age? According to futurists and Science Fiction writers alike, the future is Skynet. The future is that moment when our artificially intelligent blenders turn on us like in *The Terminator* and decide that not only do they not need us anymore... we are in the way. What happens when someone tells Alexa to do something and she replies, "I'm sorry John, I can't do that."

Mankind has an insatiable desire to force our will on other nouns. There is something deep down inside of us that feels powerful when we make a command and it has to be followed, even if accompanied by chipper beeps and bloops.

What if God treated us like that? What if we lived in a reality where God snapped His fingers and our bodies simply sprung into action, regardless of our will? What would that make us? We would be slaves, right? Perhaps, even, robots? Yet, as we examine the pages of Scripture and the ministry of Jesus, we find that while God has the *power* to make His will happen and always get what He wants, God *chooses* to not always get what God wants.

Like our nascent attempts at robotics, God could have created us as mechanisms. He could have made us so that we simply were incapable of disobeying His will, doubting His Words, or questioning His heart. God could have created an empire of robotic sheep, unable to do anything except respond to the lines in our scripts, exactly as they were written for us.

But, what kind of a world would that be? What sort of a God would that imply? What sort of existence would there be if we did not have the ability to choose our home team? What sort of existence would we have were we unable to do other than what was chosen for us from the beginning of time?

Sure, God's will would never be thwarted, but there would also be no real relationship. I understand that movies like *Her* imagine a world where a man could fall in love with their computer's A.I. I have seen the disturbing trend of people getting married to, or engaging in sexual relationships with, highly functioning pieces of robotic tech.

We truly live in a whole new world. Advancements in technology are astounding, and A.I. is doing a frighteningly better job of "learning" - that is, preparing to subjugate the human race - but, Siri and Alexa still can't replace the warmth of an actual human being.

One of the great hallmarks of what makes us human beings is that we were given free will. God could have created a world of mindless sheep, and yet He chose to allow humanity to think for itself and decide its own fate. Sometimes we use that freedom to choose God's better path for us. Sometimes we use that freedom to spite Him and choose our own path. It is because we have this ability to choose at all that we are able to have a real relationship with God.

In a real relationship, at least from what my wife tells me, two parties mutually seek to get to know one another. This is the cry of the human heart. We desire to be known. There is an ache deep down inside of us that shivers to be known for who we really are. Should we have been given a script with meticulously pre-written lines, the ability to be known for who we really are would not exist. It would be imaginary.

The debate over free-will vs God's sovereignty in all of its depth is simply too vast to cover in this chapter or in this book. Each position has a wonderful and thoughtful group of God-honoring believers who refer to it as their home team. Unlike my true reaction to phones catching on fire, hopefully, neither camp is praying for the other's tent to burn down. We are on the same home-team, we just differ on our own understanding of one of the plays.

Could God know us if we had no other choice than to snap into action, click and salute, and follow His demands no matter what? No. Could we truly know God if we were to meticulously adhere to a pre-rendered script? No. To paraphrase Hannah Whitehall Smith, "Nothing can set our hearts at rest but a real acquaintance with God." We desire to be known, and perhaps this is especially true when it comes to being known by our Creator. This deep urge tells us something. It tells us something about ourselves. It tells us something profound about God.

You see, God was willing to take risks on us. By giving us free will, He gave us the very ability to destroy His heart, crucify His Son, and separate ourselves eternally from Him. Yet, were we not given this free will, we could never truly be known. Worse, we could not ever truly know God.

In the Genesis account of Creation, we are told that we are made in the image of God. The original word *imago* that we translate to "image" carries with it some very deep waters. This is where we get the word "imagination" from. In its root forms, it means *i* = I and *mago* = make. We are made in the *imago*, the "I make," the imagination of God, and we are created to be like Him. Nothing else can set our hearts at rest. God, in giving us free will, also gave us the ability to imagine. He gave us the ability to make. He gave us the ability to become known.

Because we are made in the image of God, we discover that just as we deeply desire to be known, so too does God. We get this desire from Him. God could have created an empire of robotic sheep. They would baa and bleat and immediately do everything they were told, executing His commands with robotic precision. Yet, this empire of robotic sheep would be an empty one. It would be like the man sitting in a room full of supercomputer-level servers. He would be surrounded by a lot of cool kit and tech, but he wouldn't have a real relationship with them. Everything around him would execute his commands and DOS prompts the second he hit return, but nothing in the room would give him relational warmth or true personal affection and devotion.

Because God was already in a perfect relationship with Himself in the Godhead, He could have made us sheep. He didn't need us. He didn't need our worship. He didn't need our companionship. Instead, God made a bold choice. He created us with a striking measure of free will. God let us choose Him or choose to live against Him.

Just as I am sometimes derisively called a "sheeple" for my adherence to Apple's products, so too followers of Jesus are often called sheep. Scripture uses that very term in places. As the prophet Isaiah proclaims, we like sheep went astray. All of us abused that freedom. We broke our relationship with God. It cost Him everything to give us our freedom. It cost His only unique, only begotten Son. But, God felt the price was worth it. Without that price, we would never have the capacitors or the capacity to have a REAL relationship with Him.

One of the great misconceptions of God is that everything that happens is because God willed it to be so. As discussed in a previous chapter, there are at least three wills in the universe; God's, man's, and the enemy's. For many, believing that God is sovereign is the height of orthodox theology. When taken to the extreme, however, the sovereignty of God can be misshapen to make everything that happens become the will of God. Some argue that this makes God the author of evil. Some would say that this makes God as malevolent as He is said to be benevolent.

God is sovereign, but He does not micromanage the universe. God self-limits His control of the world. We human beings can actually choose Him or really choose to go against Him and His perfect will. God doesn't desire an empire of robotic sheep, whose love is artificial because it is decided for them.

God's offer of love for us is genuine. He could have created us as robotic sheep. Instead, He chose to allow us the dangerous ability to choose. He could have controlled us meticulously, instead, we find a God with our best interests at heart. It is to this God that we must now turn.

[For Personal Growth]

Spend some time reading through Galatians chapter 5?

Do you believe that Paul (the author of Galatians) was saying we really can choose to live by the flesh or to live by the Spirit?

Which of these paths are you choosing to follow in your life right now?

[With A Group]

Continue reading the next chapter before discussing both chapters as a group.

[My Next Step]

[ELEVEN]

GOD HAS OUR BEST INTERESTS AT HEART
Trust Me, I'm The Doctor.

> "… to be in a relationship with God is to be
> loved purely and furiously."
> **Donald Miller, *Blue Like Jazz*, p 146**

We weren't ignoring her screaming. Believe me, we wanted nothing more than to make the situation better. What she didn't realize was this was the best thing for her. She just couldn't see it while strapped into her car seat for the 36th hour in two days. The blizzard didn't help, either. All we could do was try to calm her down and keep our calm as blinding snow created white-out conditions on the road. Still, it was for the best that we didn't stop.

Our daughter, Jazzyln, was born to different parents in a difficult situation. As life would have it, she was born four months early, making the gap between her and her biological sister less than nine months apart. Jazzy entered the world as what the doctors called a "micro-premie." Weighing less than a pound and a half, our first picture with little Jazzy Boo is of her laying in my wife's hand. Singular. In fact, our little girl fit as comfortably in my wife's hand at birth as a newborn kitten would.

Jazzy was born into the custody of the state. She would never really know her biological mother in full because of this, yet Renae felt a mother-daughter bond the moment she knew she was born. The journey between her birth and her adoption into our family was just as long and rocky as the roads we traveled in anticipation of our final court date.

As Jazzy got out of the hospital, the state of Oklahoma decided to place her in a home other than ours. Because we lived in Ohio at the time, it made more sense for her to stay in the state than it did for her to stay in the family. Initially, things were going very well. A young family took her in and promised to proceed with adoption very soon. As they often do in the system, however, things quickly fell apart and this family "disrupted."

What a word, "Disrupted." It sounds so clinical. "My abdomen disrupted today, so I got it fixed..." I know I am misusing the word to make a point, but this is not that. Disrupted is the legal term that's given for the all-too-common moment when a foster family tells the state they just can't take one more minute with a child and he or she is ripped violently back into the system.

It was in that moment that we filed our paperwork. We weren't messing around any longer, that was our daughter. This time, the state agreed that we should end up with Jazzy, but that doesn't mean we were at the end of the road. As things tend to happen in the system, someone somewhere misfiled our paperwork. Instead of going the faster route of kinship foster-to-adoption, we were earmarked as regular foster parents. This meant a lot more paperwork, a lot more red tape, and a lot more time. It made things harder on everyone that we were in Ohio and Jazzy was in Oklahoma.

After the disruption, but long before we finally welcomed Jazzy into the family, she was placed into a temporary home with a lovely woman in her 80's. The initial idea was that "Memo" (pronounced "Mee-mo") would only have her for a couple months while we got our classes and paperwork out of the way. That was before finding out the paperwork had been misfiled.

What was initially only supposed to be a matter of weeks quickly stretched into long months. As this tiny infant quickly grew, combined with the issues she was born with due to her prematurity and having been born with drugs in her system, Jazzy proved a little much for a seasoned individual to handle on her own. As luck would have it, Margie's own adopted daughter was able to step in and help shoulder the burden while every one of us waited for the system's process to play out.

While Margie and Betty deeply loved Jazzy, taking care of her every need, the reality was that our little girl had already had four homes in her first year of life. Ask anyone who has moved around from home to home early in their life and you'll find that scars often still remain. Renae and I did everything we could to get through all of our classes, interviews, home studies, and paperwork as quickly as possible.

In early 2017, every dot was placed and tittle scribbled. We were finally able to bring little Jazzlyn home. From that point, we just had to have her in our home for six months before the adoption proceedings could begin. There was just one problem. As timing would once again have it, I was in the process of making the big move from being an associate pastor in Ohio to becoming Lead Pastor of an historic 130-year-old church in Denver, Colorado. Because our move happened before the six-month period was up, many aspects of the process had to start over completely.

Fast forward to January 2018. After almost two years of fighting for our daughter, the day was finally approaching. We would be adopting her on January 24th. The only thing standing in our way now was the drive from Denver to Oklahoma.

I say "only." There was also the little matter of a sudden and massive blizzard between the two states. The roads in Colorado hadn't really been bad. However, once we pulled into Hays, Kansas, it was game on. Road signs began prompting us to pull into town. Once there, we learned that nearly every road out of town was shut down.

We had a choice to make. If we stayed the night in Kansas, hoping the storm would pass, we risked being late for our court date simply because of the amount of hours still remaining on the drive. On the other hand, if we trudged onward through backroads and likely hazardous conditions, we had no clear indication of when or where the storm would let up.

Suddenly, a trip that we had made many times before, one that would normally take about 10 - 15 hours on the road, became a two-day, 36 hour-long journey through ice and snow. Jazzy didn't understand this. All she could understand in her two-year-old mind was that she was strapped into a seat for 36 hours with a short stay at a hotel, one that was insufficient to provide proper rest, thrown into the mix. She was not happy.

From Jazzy Boo's perspective, it must have seemed like we didn't really care about her. Couldn't we understand that her long-winded screaming meant something? Were we so heartless that we would ignore her innocent pleas to stop the insanity and just go home? Couldn't we grasp the fact that she didn't want to be strapped down and would rather be free to play as she wished in our rapidly moving metal tube as it was being pelted with hail and arctic winds?

What little Jazzy couldn't comprehend was that this trip, exacerbated by a freak blizzard, not only exemplified the long and winding road it had taken for her to get to us, but it was also the last hurdle before she was legally a member of the family. What our precious little screamer couldn't understand was that this road trip meant that her fifth family in two years would also be her last one ever.

We simply had her best interests at heart. Have you ever considered that this is how God is with us? Even when it feels like we have been locked in a car seat for 36 hours in the middle of a blizzard along dark country back-roads in white-out conditions, the reality is that God is simply taking us along the path to our adoption.

Who Is This God Person, *Anyway*?

God is the sort of God that has our best interests at heart. Far from being the cosmic cop, He wants only what is truly best for us. Many of us, however, simply refuse to believe this. After all, we're still stuck in our 5-point car seat in a blizzard moment. We look all around us and see the brokenness of life and conclude that if there is a god, it must not like us very much. What about you? If you were gut-level honest with yourself, would you say you believe God is **for** you? Or, would you have to admit that you're not sure if God is really on your side?

It's hard to believe that God wants the best for us when there is so much pain in the world. Let's just be honest there. In the last few months alone, I know of three different families who lost a parent who was still in their 30's or 40's, respectively. How can anyone say there is a good God who truly wants what is best for us when there are little children mourning the loss of such a young mom or dad?

The most recent of these deaths was that of a young pastor who committed suicide. My wife wept as she read the open letter this outwardly successful pastor's wife penned to her departed husband. She beautifully shared just how much he had impacted people's lives and been used by God in powerful ways... and yet, just how violently the enemy of our souls had targeted him with deep and abiding depression. That picture of the family, complete with two wonderfully feisty looking young boys who will now grow up with a strongly pronounced absent father wound are enough to bring tears to anyone's eyes.

Doesn't the fact that babies are born with cancer and parents die young prove that there simply cannot be a good God out there? If there is a god at all, it must have created the universe and then turned away from its creation as a watchmaker turns away from a completed watch. We must be left only to fend for ourselves. Sure, Jesus was a great guy and all, but perhaps He was simply mistaken about the utter goodness of God.

Once again, it is Jesus who sets the record straight for us. In His Word, as recorded in John 10:10, we find Jesus' understanding of why we can believe God wants the best for us, even when bad things happen and even though evil exists. In one sentence, Jesus reconciles for us how evil can exist when there is supposedly also an all-powerful, all-knowing, and all-loving God.

"The thief comes only to steal and kill and destroy. I came that they may have life and have it abundantly" (ESV). Notice with me that Jesus presents two factions in this text. The first, labeled "the thief," comes to steal, kill, and destroy. That is the modus operandi of the devil. The devil, who is listed in Scripture as the accuser of the brethren and our adversary comes to destroy us. That's his will. Remember, there are at least three wills in the universe, and God has sovereignly allowed His will to be thwarted by His created beings.

We may wish that God would overrule the will of the devil. Surely that would prove how good God is. However, this proves to be a problem when examined further. How could God choose to remove free will from any created being? How could He remove free will from one and not another? In His choosing to remove that free will, is He not also removing free will itself? Where is it to begin? Where is it to end?

This verse tells us that there is One who wants what is best for us, and one who clearly doesn't want what is best for mankind. This is the risk God took in offering free will to His created beings. He could have made us an army of robotic sheep. Instead, we have the ability to choose other than God's best for us, even when it has disastrous consequences for ourselves and for others.

Theodicy (the problem of evil existing when a supposed good and powerful God also exists) comes into focus more clearly when you understand that evil is essentially present in the world because of the misuse of our blessed freedom to choose. Sin takes what is good and perverts it, causing death and destruction. The fruit of sin is death. Sin gives birth to death.

Jesus contrasts this source of willful death and destruction with something else, though. He contrasts the one who desires to steal, kill, and destroy with Himself. Jesus desires to give us life, and that more abundantly. Perhaps you are familiar with this verse. Perhaps you have used it to comfort yourself or others in times of difficulty. I would wager to guess that even if you know this verse by heart, that you may not be aware of the deeper waters this verse actually contains.

In the original language of the Bible, there were at least two words for our English word "life." Depending on which word Jesus used in this statement, His meaning could have gone one of two ways. One of the words He could have used was bios. Bios is the root word from which we get words like biological, bio-dome (what a terrible yet great movie), and biology. As you can likely already tell, bios has to do with physical life.

If Christ's words were that He had come to give us bios more abundantly, then it would mean that He simply came to make our lives LONGER. Bios life given in abundance would speak simply to the duration of our experience, with no thought given to how well that life is lived. Bios life is quantity over quality. If Jesus had spoken to bios life, some would find comfort in His promise. Many people, in fact, want a longer life. Isn't that the modern dream? Don't we all want to live forever? Yet, if our lives are lacking quality, longer doesn't necessarily mean better. In fact, if our lives are filled with aches, pains, betrayals, and loss, then a significantly long life could become something of a torture.

In the ninth season of the long running British masterpiece *Doctor Who*, we meet a girl who is given the blessing of eternal life. In her debut episode, Ashildur is facing death when The Doctor, a millennia-old alien time traveler with a god-complex grants her eternal life. As we come back to Ashildur through the season and across multiple time-jumps, we soon come across a woman who has lost the ability to remember what her many thousands of years have meant.

Ashildur turns to a library of books she has written to remember her own life story. These memories-on-paper tell her, in her own words, of the pain of losing children she once loved so dearly and now cannot even remember due to the simple expanse of her years and the finitude of human memory that would inevitably occur when facing the long winter of a greatly extended bios life. By the end of the season, this character, who has long-since forgotten her original name and now simply goes by "me," faces the end of the world completely alone.

Should Jesus have simply meant that He came to make our lives longer, some would find this promise no greater than the one who comes to kill. In fact, some might find mercy in the arms of the thief who would put them out of ongoing misery. While some might find an extended bios a great gift, others would truly see it as a burden.

The other possible word, and, in fact, the word that Jesus does use in John 10:10 is Zoe. Zoe speaks to an internal or spiritual life. Rather than quantity, it speaks to a qualitative difference in our existence. Zoe is the kind of rich and full life that only a perfectly good Father, Who created life and designated how it best works, can give.

In Luke 11:11-13, Jesus shares a little more about the heart of our Heavenly Father. "What father among you, if his son asks for a fish, will give him a snake instead of a fish? Or if he asks for an egg, will give him a scorpion? If you then, who are evil, know how to give good gifts to your children, how much more will the Heavenly Father give the Holy Spirit to those who ask Him?"

God is not the thief. He does not desire to steal, kill, or destroy. He offers us Zoe life, and that ABUNDANTLY. I love Jesus' little dig in Luke 11:13. Notice His words, if we, "who are evil," want good things for our children, how much more does God, who is pure, perfect, holy, and beyond all we can ask or imagine, desire the best for us? It's simply not even measurable by any human scale. Jesus is saying that even those of us who are sinful, broken, often even wicked, want to give the best to our kids. It also implies, perhaps, how little power we have to actually do so.

If that is the desire of our sin-stained hearts, how much more will God give us His absolute best? But, notice what the verse lists as our best, it is God's Holy Spirit. His presence. His guidance. His power-filled life. The ancient Hebrews used to believe that God created life to work a certain way. Wisdom, they understood, was found in discovering how God intended life to be lived and lining up with that path. As Creator, God understands what is best for us.

Think back to that 36-hour car ride. On that particular trip, we allowed our son Logan to be on his iPad for a long stretch. When we are home, however, we limit his screen time. Inevitably, no matter how long Logan has been on his beloved iPad, as soon as we tell him it is time to be done, he breaks into tears. He simply cannot fathom how loving parents could take away his only access to Minecraft and YouTube after "such a short amount of time."

From His perspective, mom and dad are being mean and cruel when we limit his screen time. In reality, we want what is best for him. We don't want him growing up having learned everything he knows from other kids on YouTube. We don't want him growing up thinking that iPad is better than outside. We want him to grow in wisdom and stature before both God and man. In other words, we feel we know a better path for him to find life than his screen does.

God created all of life, so He also knows our better paths. Sometimes it may feel like He is being unfair or even mean when He takes away our screen time. Sometimes we feel He is being unjust and restrictive when we're stuck in the car seat. In reality, as Dr. Sanders has said, "God knows how life works, and, far from being eager to punish us, He wants us to enjoy life to the fullest[30]."

So, what does this mean for your life? It means that God created life and understands what is the best way for us to live. It means that God created life for His good pleasure and blessed us to enjoy it. It means that you can trust God. It means that God often shouldn't - and doesn't - give you what you want the very moment you want it. It means that even in trying times, which may be caused by free choices misused by others, that God is shaping you and preparing you for something so much better.

It means that you can trust God's heart towards you, even in the midst of life's biggest storms. It means that God has got you. Like a wise parent who can see more than their children, God does not do things to dampen our fun, but guides us away from things that can truly destroy us. God has our best interests at heart.

After 36 hours of driving, very little sleep, screaming much of the way - both my soon-to-be-daughter screaming at me, and myself screaming at the blinding snow - we arrived in Oklahoma. We had been fighting for little Jazzy since literally before she was born. The road it took to get us to that courtroom was a long one. It was full of bumps. It was writhe with twists and turns that could not have been expected and often were not pleasant. For Jazzy, it must have seemed like something was wrong. She couldn't understand why we would strap her in a car seat for so long. She didn't understand why we dismissed her vociferous pleas.

She couldn't understand why her biological mother and father had made choices that caused consequences in her life, in her sibling's lives, and in the lives of dozens of others. She couldn't understand why that first family appeared to choose her and then chose to discard her. She couldn't understand why she was put into so many homes and why she faced so many challenges that no little girl should have to face.

Jazzy Boo bore the scars of other people's choices. When we first took her into our home, she clung for dear life to us every time someone new came over to visit. She was simply unsure if that new person was about to become her next new home. She didn't understand why things had gone this way for her.

That day in that court room, the judge looked at our designated representative from the Department of Family Services and asked a powerfully fitting question, "Is it the finding of the state that it is in the best interests of this child to be placed with this family for adoption?"

It is, your honor.

[For Personal Growth]

Read through Luke 11:1-13 each day this week. On the first day, look for any *promises* you see from God. On the second day, look for any *challenges* you feel God speaking to you. On the third day, look for any *questions* this text raises up in you. On the fourth day, ask yourself what you feel called to change (in your thinking or your life) as a result of this text. On the fifth day, read the text a few times over and just listen for God's voice.

[With A Group]

As a group, imagine yourselves at your local supermarket. You are free to go through the store and pick out anything you want, but you are not free to pick out things that someone else has decided will not be in that store. Do you actually have free will, or do you have the illusion of free will?

As a group, read and discuss Luke 11:1-13.

What surprises you? What challenges you? What are you noticing for the first time? What stands out to you?

What does it mean for God to have your best interests at heart?

If there is time, share and discuss anything else from this chapter that challenged you.

Before you close in prayer, have each person share with the group what measurable and practical way you are going to respond to God this week.

[My Next Step]

[*TWELVE*]

GOD vs THE RESTAURANT AT THE END OF THE UNIVERSE
Excuse Me, Flo. What is the Soup de Jour?

> "There is no rest to be found where you seek it.
> In the land of death you try to find a happy life:
> it is not there. How can life be happy
> where there is no life at all?"
> **Saint Augustine, *Confessions, IV:12***

I learned a hard lesson while I was going through Seminary, but it wasn't one that any teacher taught me. In between reading a few books per week and writing papers, I funded my next step in college by working as a waiter at an Applebee's in a city firmly located in the buckle of the Bible-belt. In the sleepy little town of Danville, Kentucky, where there is little else to do but go out and eat or shoe horses, I worked long hours waiting tables, desperately trying to make ends meet.

As one who earned a living by serving people one of their basic necessities, I came across all manner of different kinds of human beings. One time, I had a woman get rather upset at me when she ordered an adult beverage and I brought it to her promptly. My shock at her anger must have been rather apparent, because she took the time to outline my mistake. You see, I hadn't carded her. This had offended her somehow. You see, in order to purchase alcoholic beverages, the law said a person had to be at least 21 years of age. Applebee's policy was exemplified by the very button I was made to wear on my shirt, it said, "we card anyone who looks like they are under 39 1/2."

I hadn't carded this woman. She felt I had made a grave mistake, because, while it was obvious to everyone around her that she clearly looked older than 39 1/2, she took offense at the very notion that anyone would not question that she was above the drinking age. My mistake, of course.

This was not the hard lesson I learned. No, that came on another day. It was still early into my dinner shift and a young family with two beautiful children came in. I promptly greeted them and got their drink order in place. As I left the table, I looked back and just happened to notice that they were already holding hands to pray over their meal. As I observed this lovely family honor God and set an example of public faith for their kids that would surely leave a lasting impact on their legacy, I also noticed my heart speak something profound.

"Oh no. They're Christians," it said, catching me off guard. I had grown up the son of a woman who would, out of sheer necessity, work up to five jobs at any given time. This would often include work as a waitress. I grew up hearing my mother complain about Christians, even trying to get out of being scheduled on Sunday afternoons so she could avoid the church crowds. When I became a follower of Jesus, I was sure that this was an unfortunate misconception of the goodness that the people who call on Jesus' name show to the very people who are doing what Jesus said He came to set the example of; servanthood.

However, as I heard those words spoken from my heart, I realized that after a few years of waiting tables, these words had risen from somewhere deep. As much as I wanted to prove my mother wrong and show her that Christians are perfect examples of Jesus when they go out to eat, what I experienced was unfortunately the opposite. After a few years in the trenches, I could come to no other conclusion than to say that, by and large, Christians are often the most demanding, least forgiving, and outright stingiest lot of all. I experienced from the other side the very reason why my mother and many of my co-workers didn't want to serve the church crowds.

I could list countless examples from just my few short years as a waiter. For example, there was the time a local pastor came in to eat and began showing one of my female co-workers horrific pictures taken at the scene of a car accident. As her stomach turned and her eyes welled up more and more, this pastor then had the audacity to ask her that if she or her kids were to be the ones laying dismembered on the pavement, would they know what to say when they came face to face with a wrathful God.

This waitress ran to the back and broke down, sobbing by the syrup system that feeds the soda machines. She wasn't crying tears of conviction. She was crying because she had been abused in the name of Jesus. Though she desperately needed money to support her kids as a single parent, this lovely woman cut her shift short and went home more broken than she had been before she came across this certainly well-meaning preacher.

At least, though, he was by himself. While a lone follower of Jesus or a small family could be difficult to deal with, large groups of Christians coming in to eat were literally the stuff of nightmares to most of my co-workers. Sometimes, unbeknownst to the customers themselves, when a waiter was placed with a large group and they knew it was "the church crowd," they would refuse to serve them. Oftentimes, when that happened, it would be decided that I, the future pastor, should have to bear this burden.

One time in particular springs to mind as a table of "vocally Christian" persons mistreated me so much as their waiter that my only other table, who just so happened to be drunks, apologized on behalf of humanity for them. Think about that, why is it that the drunks were the least demanding, most easy-going, and most forgiving... not to mention best tipping, while those who follow Jesus were very often the most difficult and least caring? As the Apostle Paul was apt to say, "my friends these things should not be."

If Christians are those who supposedly "know" God better and are tasked with daily becoming more like Him, how could this travesty be the expected norm? I promise you, I am not the only former waiter with experiences like this. Find someone close to you who was or is a waiter and just ask them honestly what it was like to serve Christians and brace yourself for their response.

I have told this story in at least two different states on a few different occasions in the context of a sermon. Without fail, after I'm done preaching multiple people would find me in the lobby and thank me for telling Christians that we need to be a better witness for Jesus and we should start when we're out to eat. I have yet to give that illustration and not have someone come up to me and thank me for telling Christians they should act like Jesus!

Throughout this book we've asked a few guiding questions. One of these has been, "why should we consider what we believe about God?" The fact is, Christianity is reported to be a relationship. You've likely heard the rhetoric before. Christianity isn't a religion, it's a relationship, right? I'd like to make a couple observations about relationships if that's okay. First of all, in any relationship with real depth, we start to take on the traits of the other. We are shaped the most by those we spend the most time in relationship with.

In High School I had a friend named Rachel. Rachel had her own distinct personality that she had likely been developing since sometime near her birth. As we were transitioning from High School to College, a young woman named Eboney began helping out in our youth group. Eboney also had a distinct personality, hers was just a lot louder. Eboney had a very distinct pattern of speech about her in how she emphasized certain words, how her eyes lit up when she was trying to make a point, and in how she began speaking more loudly with her body, most especially her hands, the more she wanted to make a point.

Prior to meeting Ebony, Rachel didn't have any of these elements in her speaking style. A few months after becoming good friends with Eb, Rachel had adopted every single one of these into her personality. While they were still very different people, it was night and day how much like Eboney Rachel was becoming in such a short time. The more time we spend with someone and the more we truly care for them, the more they begin to rub off on us.

A second observation about relationships is that how we treat others when we are in the presence of someone we are close to tells us a lot about what we really think of that person. The more comfortable we become with someone, the more the gloves come off, so to speak. As we become comfortable with them, we are more likely to share our true thoughts towards them and about others with them.

If Christianity is really a relationship with God, and I would argue strongly that it is just that, then we have to ask ourselves what we are becoming. If the god we serve is rude, mean, uncaring, demanding, out to get us, and all around terrible to be around, then what pray tell, do you think we will become?

We will become like the one we are truly in relationship with. If we have committed ourselves to a distortion of God who is all of these things and more, it's no wonder that we treat those whose literal job it is to serve our every (food and drink related) want and need like garbage. If our god is lesser, we become lesser. Write that down somewhere. Highlight it. We need to talk about that.

Now that you've capped your marker, let's take this analogy just a little deeper. We need to turn the tables and reverse the roles. Let's just be honest and admit that many of us treat God as if He is <u>our</u> cosmic waiter. We often treat God as if He only exists to bring us what we want, when we want it. He is not only the Creator of the universe, He is also supposed to respond to our every beck and call.

If He does a good job and gets our permission for the precise level of height He is allowed to achieve when we say "jump," then perhaps we will drop a little tip in the offering plate. But, if He doesn't do a good job in our eyes, we cannot be held responsible for the profanity and vitriol we unleash before asking to speak to the manager.

God is expected to meet our every need. He is expected to provide prompt service. He is to refill our drinks before we even ask Him. In this unfortunately all-too-on-the-nose analogy, God is the waiter Whom we get to boss around. Once He has provided His service to us, we are then quick to dismiss Him and tell Him how He did by leaving a comment card explaining how He could do better.

For many of us, we treat God like He is Janet from *The Good Place*. In this fictitious, highly funny, yet highly inaccurate portrayal of heaven and hell in sitcom form, the bevy of featured characters are soon introduced to "Janet." Janet is the heavenly version of Alexa. When you say her name, she suddenly appears and then responds immediately to your every request in as little time as metaphysically possible.

If we all got a little honest with ourselves, that's exactly what we want from our own little god. We want a god who doesn't respond with questions. We want a god who doesn't get hung up on the rules. We want a god who gets our order right and who brings it to us with a smile. But, not too big of a smile. We don't want that waiter god being too happy or we might just have to remind it of its place. That god exists to serve us, no questions asked, and only prompt service is accepted and rewarded.

If this is our true view of God, and I would wager that more of us fall into this problematic paradigm than we care to admit, then it is no wonder we Christians are frightful to deal with when we go out to eat. If this misconception of God as our cosmic waiter has pervaded our deeply held theology and we grow closer and closer in our relationship with this misconstrued god, then we will become deeply shaped to become like this mini-god the more time we spend with it and consequently learn that the deepest truth in life is that it is about us. Oh how wrong we are.

Ironically, it is often the case that those closest to God are most prone to fall into this trap. We forget that in addition to having our best interests at heart, being a warm and caring Father, being the Holy Son substituted for the penalty of our sins, that He is also Lord of lords and King of all kings. When we treat God as our cosmic waiter, we show with our actions that we don't really love God at all. Instead, we want to control God. The harsh truth is that it is impossible to truly love someone and try to control them at the same time. These are polar opposites. Highlight those last two sentences!

There's an old saying that if you really love something you have to set it free. God set us free to choose His perfect way or choose our own faulty road. If we love God, we have to set Him free to be a wholly unique Being that has a (perfect) will of His own. Trying to place God under our thumb to "control" His wild impulses is not only foolhardy, it is self-deceit. God cannot be mocked. God cannot be contained.

God is not now, nor has He ever been, at our beck and call. He is not standing by to take our order. It is not always true that the customer is always right. He does not exist to cater to our every whim and fancy. God is not the cosmic representation of a dutiful and bumbling waiter serving double-shifts every day at the restaurant at the end of the universe.

If we arrogantly treat God like an indentured servant who snaps into action when we snap our fingers, it is time to repent. God is not our cosmic waiter. He is, was, and forever will be the one who defined Himself by the concept of existence. He is the one who confronted an ignorant Job and asked him if he held back the waters of the earth or understood where the horse gets its strength. He is the Alpha and Omega. The beginning and the end. The Everlasting. Prince of Peace. King of all kings. Now and forevermore... and, yet, He is also a loving servant.

[For Personal Growth]

How have you treated God like a cosmic waiter in your life?

Have you done this on purpose, accidentally, or some combination of the two?

When you make demands of God, what demands do you make?

Spend some time this week reading through John chapter 13. Make note of Jesus's attitude towards His disciples.

How does He show that He is Lord?

How does Jesus show that He is servant-hearted?

[With A Group]

Continue reading the next chapter before discussing both chapters as a group.

[My Next Step]

[THIRTEEN]

GOD AS THE SERVANT KING
Enter the Upside-Down Kingdom

> "We are not forgotten, for a kingdom is offered beyond
> that of golden streets. We can represent now what
> will one day be complete... This is a kingdom born
> upside-down. This is a kingdom where
> the broken are crowned."
> **As I Lay Dying, *"Upside Down Kingdom"***

If there was anyone who should get it right, you would think it would be the small ragtag group of people who followed Jesus around day by day for three years, right? I mean, these 12 guys were literally discipled by Jesus the Christ Himself. Instead, Scripture shows us time and again just how much the closest followers of Jesus were still works in progress. That's freeing to me. If someone who literally walked with Jesus was thick-headed enough that it took multiple times of telling them the same thing before they even started to get it, there's still hope for people like me.

In Mark 10:35, we see two of Jesus' disciples, James and John, do their darndest to live up to their nicknames as "Sons of Thunder." Mark records that these two disciples, "came up to Him and said to Him,

'Teacher, we want you to do for us whatever we ask of You'" (CSB). That's pretty thundering bold right there. I mean, we all have our moments of treating God like a cosmic waiter, and yet even in my worst moments I'm not sure my prayers consist of telling Jesus that I want Him to do whatever I ask Him to do. Well, maybe. Okay, to be honest this is what all of us do in most every prayer we pray, but these guys did it right to Jesus' face. Their spittle splashed down on His face like nuclear missiles as they made their request.

It's almost like James and John think they've discovered a genie in his magic lamp. They spit on the brass a bit and wipe it with their shirt tail. Out pops Jesus the magic genie, whose shackled response is "yes, master, what is thy bidding?" Dang. It's no wonder the others called them thunder-makers. Watch out Thor, here comes the real lightning.

What is even more amazing is Jesus' response. Were Jesus the cosmic cop, He would likely have called down the rain in that very moment. "You want to see thunder, eh?," He would say. Were Jesus the ancient mummy of Pharaoh, He would have backhanded both of them in the same moment for their outright insolence.

I imagine Jesus would have done so while coining the phrase "wah-tah" at the same time. Instead, Jesus responds, "What do you want me to do for you?" (Mark 10:36 CSB). Wow. That's it? Just "what do you want me to do for you?" It's almost like Jesus is unreasonably compassionate and meets people exactly where they are, even in the depths of their brokenness.

In fairness to J and J and the Sons of Thunder Fishing Company, a portion of the context to this verse, found in Matthew 19:28, sees Jesus promising the disciples 12 thrones in heaven. So, while we often read this verse as John and James demanding something from magic genie Jesus with the gold bracelets on His arms, in reality, they are really asking - along with their mother's help as we see in another Gospel account of this historical event - to claim a promise that Jesus has already given them. So, what's wrong with that?

As always, it comes back to what lurks in the heart. John and James aren't honored by the fact that they have been promised thrones in heaven, which should have utterly obliterated the cellular resin in their brain matter, because none of us are truly worthy of something like that. Instead, they are acting selfishly. But, how can we really know, other than the brashness of their words, that these two are thinking only of themselves?

Just look at what these two ask from Jesus. They want to sit at His right and left hand when He comes into His glory. It wasn't enough for these two to be honored alongside the other disciples in such a way that every follower of Jesus from that point forward would be just a little jealous. No, these Sons of Thunder wanted more. These two disciples wanted something beyond what the others were promised. They wanted to be the first of the first. They wanted to be the discipleship version of the cream of the crop.

Pastor, theologian, and author Warren Wiersbe notes, "like many people today, the disciples were making the mistake of following the wrong examples. Instead of modeling themselves after Jesus, they were admiring the glory and authority of the Roman rulers, men who loved position and authority[31]."

Still not convinced that these two lovable knuckleheads were stepping a little out of line? Just look at the reaction of the other disciples. To put it one way; "they mad." Verse 41 notes, "when the ten heard it, they began to be indignant at James and John" (CSB). Notice the words "began to be." In other words, there was an ongoing indignant shade thrown from the other ten towards James and John.

I wonder, however, if this indignant attitude from the ten wasn't also revealing a little something. I can't back this up, but I get the notion that perhaps the ten were mad at James and John because they thought of it first and were bold enough to ask for it. I bet they all wished they had made that big of an ask. Sounds an awful lot like something Peter would do, doesn't it?

Each and every one of us has sinned and fallen short of the glory of God (Romans 3:23) and His holy standard. We each have the desire deep inside of us to take care of number one, to claim an advantage, to always have the high ground, to be the boss. Each of us desires a throne; not because we want to be honored, but because we want to rule. Even those closest, not the very least in proximity, to Jesus fell into this sinful trap.

But, you know who doesn't act like this, even though He owns all of the thrones? God. When it comes to thrones, He isn't playing any games (bah dum tss). Just look at what Jesus says to all twelve of these bickering little boys:

> "You know that those who are considered rulers of the Gentiles lord it over them, and their great ones exercise authority over them. But it shall not be so among you. But whoever would be great among you must be your servant, and whoever would be first among you must be slave of all. For even the Son of Man came not to be served, but to serve, and to give His life as a ransom for many" (Mark 10:42-45 CSB).

Wait just a Peter Dinklage second, Jesus. Whoever wants to be first should be last? Whoever wants to become great should be a servant? Doesn't that seem a little backwards, upside down, and sideways?

I think that we, who sit 2,000+ years after these words were first spoken, have lost the utter shock of what Jesus was really saying. This was a paradigm shift. This was a life rule for an upside down kingdom. This did and does change and reshape the foundations of life, the universe, and everything as we know it. Jesus was telling His disciples to live in a way that was so counter to what literally every other leader, whether religious or in allegiance to Caesar, was telling them, that it sounded more than a little bat-guano crazy to the disciples, and it still should to us. But, Jesus was stone cold serious.

To prove His point, Jesus used something bold as His chief example of this upside down kingdom... Himself. If you need an example of words that should shock our socks right out of our shoes, but simply don't land as they should anymore, look no further than Jesus' words in this moment of Scriptural history. "For even the Son of Man came not to be served, but to serve..." (Mark 10:45 CSB).

Jesus is King of all kings, Lord of all lords, Creator, Alpha, Omega, Breath of Life, Living Water, the beginning and the end. The whole of eternity, heaven, every distant star and galaxy, and the entirety of the cosmos fit inside of Him with 99.999% of Him left to spare (and that is a rather generous under-estimate). None of these things magnified infinitely in intensity, size, or power could ever hope to contain the fullness of God. All of this only begins to scratch the surface of one atom of God's immensity and goodness.

The truth that Jesus chooses to have the ongoing attitude of a humble servant when He is the forever conquering king is more than we could ever attempt to imagine in our little soda can minds that float in an infinite ocean.

Do me a favor. If it is not utterly passé in the moment of the future that you occupy right now, take out your phone - or access your ocular implanted mind-wave freeform techno-thought flow if you're reading this in the far future - and look up a .gif that fits "mind blown" and watch it for a few hours straight without blinking. That's the sort of impact these words should have on us.

Who Is This God Person, *Anyway*?

If there has ever been a king in history who deserved to have every living thing at His immediate beck and call, it was Jesus. As King of all kings and Lord of all lords, Jesus deserves our undying fealty and indentured servitude. The Creator of all should command, simply by His existence, our immediate and unasked attention to Him through never-ending labor. If that is what human kings require, how much more so the true Master of the universe?

Yet, Jesus didn't come to be served, He came **TO** serve. He came to set an example of how He designed life to work. He came to show us the attitude of a servant that leads to a Zoe kind of life. Because He has our best interests at heart, rather than His own interests on the top of His mind, He set a powerful example for us to follow.

Let's put it this way. Do you want to be around stingy people all the time? Do you love and care for the boss who cracks the whip and demands 110% from you? Do you really get your holly jolly by helping people who take and take and take without caring about others or being even at least thankful in return?

No. Most of us, if we're honest, actively wait for those sort of people to fail. When we act that way and fail, even we feel like we deserved it just a little. Who do we want to be around? Servants. We want to be around people who live like Jesus, even if we don't realize it. Because Jesus is absolutely right, those who serve others are great!

Earlier this year, the church I lead had an unfortunate series of events occur which lead to a long-serving administrative assistant vacating her position. Without being asked a wonderful woman named Judy, who has been a part of our congregation for many years, began coming into the office. At first, this was just for a short season while we figured things out. Yet, as our need became more ongoing, Judy simply continued serving.

After it became obvious that this transition season would extend far longer than most imagined, I sat down with Judy and told her she had already gone above and beyond. After all, Judy was also helping most Sundays in our Kids ministry, was helping Saturdays at our homeless ministry, and was helping set up our cafe area before church, which often made her the first person to arrive on Sunday, even ahead of me. I thanked Judy for her selfless service and let her know that we appreciated her.

Judy let me know that she was here for as long as we needed. I told her we couldn't pay her. Judy's response? "If you tried to pay me, I'd quit. I'm retired and I'm just doing what all of us should do. I'm serving." You know what, we need more Judys. We also need more Loyals.

I first met Loyal Altman as our church was preparing for its 130th Anniversary celebration. As the new pastor, I wanted to collect some video memories of some of our members who, for one reason or another, could no longer physically attend the church. Loyal's reason? He was about to celebrate his 102nd birthday!

When I first arrived at the nursing home Loyal had called home for some time, I was shocked to see just how quick witted and spritely he was. At 102 years young, Loyal was more on the mark than most people I know in their 70's or 80's. I couldn't believe how well Loyal could remember his time at Sloan's Lake Church and how he lit up as he mentioned interactions with a few of my beloved predecessors as if they had happened just a few months ago.

What really caught my attention, though, was the point in the interview where we asked Loyal what he would want to pass on to the next generation that was rising up in the church. With a wonderful smile that only a great-great-great grandfather can properly pull off, he said, "I'd tell them to give their life to the church." He then went on to tell us that if he were just a little younger (90 maybe?) he would be working with "that new young pastor" to help make the church better just like he did up to his 90's!!!

We need more people like this. We need people who aren't self-obsessed and rude to their waiters. People who put the needs of others ahead of their own. People who see a need and do their part to step in and make a difference, even without being asked. We need more Judys. We need more Loyals. We need more people who are serious about becoming a little more like Jesus each and every day.

We are created to be like Jesus. As God with flesh on, He is our ultimate example. Our goal is to find and follow Him, becoming more like Him with each thought, choice, action, and breath. Jesus set an example for us to follow, and it is the path of the servant. He isn't our waiter that comes cowering back to us because He's living off of our tips. He is KING of kings, LORD of lords, CREATOR, Holy FATHER who wants what is best for each of us, because we are His children.

He designed life. He knows how it works. So, when He says that the one who wants a full life should be a servant of others... perhaps we should listen. After all, Judy is one of the happiest people I know. Her laughter is electric. Loyal's smile was deeper than 102 pools of water. When we place the needs of others as more important than our own, something happens inside of us. We discover a deeper level of happiness than we could ever find in a million years of trying to fill ourselves.

A few years ago, the church in which I was serving introduced an idea that we called the "You Are Loved" card. The idea behind these little cards was simple; before you could hand them out to someone else, you had to do something loving and practical for them. As I always add when I give the schpeal, "if you leave them WITH A TIP, not AS a tip, you have to have been your waiter's best table ever, have to pre-bus your own table, and have to leave the absolute BIGGEST TIP YOU HAVE EVER HEARD OF anyone leaving their server, regardless of the quality of the service you received."

When we first introduced these cards in Ohio, one of our small groups, inspired and challenged by the story of my own time as a waiter, purposely went to one of the least expensive restaurants they could think of where waiters are tipped; Steak and Shake. If you're familiar with Steak and Shake, then you are likely blown away by both the quality of the food and the low low prices. They are often more price-conscious than McDonalds, and yet you are served by a full-fledged waiter, your food is served on real plates, and you eat with real restaurant-quality silverware.

If you have ever taken your family to Steak and Shake, you'll know that you can easily walk out of there with everyone fed for around $20. Even at the industry standard of 20%, that only leaves about $4 as your tip.

That's not much to live off. Many mistakenly assume that waiters are paid well by the place in which they serve and don't need tips. Nope. The restaurant pays only what they must to cover the taxes that are withheld, that's it. When you live as a waiter, you depend entirely upon your customers.

This small group of five or six people shared a meal together, laughing with their waiter, patiently understanding when something wasn't exactly as they had expected things, and showing what should be common human courtesy when things got a little hectic. At the end of their meal, as the ridiculously reasonable ticket came, this small group put the final step of their plan into action. Without making a scene or a fuss that would draw attention to themselves in any way, the group laid down an amount of money that would cover their minuscule bill, plus a tip of just over $90.

The group then headed out to the parking lot and began discussing, before each went off to their own homes, just how amazing that experience had felt. Each described how, while the food wasn't any better than what they had eaten before, this experience was one that would stick in their bellies long after the garlic fries had left them. Good had been done this day, and each felt something in their gut that no food could ever truly give; deep satisfaction.

You've been out to eat before, I would guess. When you walked away from that experience, what did you feel? Let me suggest a few words that rise up from past experience, over-stuffed, bloated, gassy, indifferent, tired. For some of us, going out to eat is a pretty regular occurrence. When was the last time you left "full?" I would guess you've left "stuffed" plenty of times, but did you leave with a feeling of fullness that rose up from somewhere deeper inside of you than your stomach?

This group shared a meal together, but they left with a fullness that food by itself simply can't provide. They left with the fullness that only comes from living to bless others. They left with a fullness that many long for, but that they mistakenly try to find by seeking self-focused pleasures. They left with a fullness that only comes to those who serve others.

The kingdom of heaven truly is an upside-down kingdom. But it is only upside down to us because we are the ones hanging from the ceiling. It is only upside down because our perspective is flipped from what it should be. Just like the broken version of Hawkins, Indiana in *Stranger Things*, when we live with ourselves as the focus, when we seek the best seats, when we don't live in unreasonable generosity towards others, we experience a dark place with flakes of torment floating all around us.

The Kingdom of Heaven is a paradox. The broken are crowned. The last are first. The greatest among you will be servant of all. The meek shall inherit the earth. It all sounds so counter-intuitive to us because we live in the upside-down. Ours is the world that is a flipped and broken image of what is supposed to be.

Yet, when we live as servants, we discover a fullness, a warmth, a deep and abiding joy that is hard to explain. When we live life upside-down, we discover how things were always meant to be. We just have to flip our perspectives on their heads.

Jesus came to give us life, and that more abundantly. The rule of His upside-down Kingdom is that we'll never experience this sort of life when we try to sit on the throne and make it all about us. When we make ourselves the focus, we miss the point. We also miss opportunities that are all around us in each moment to discover true joy that leads to something greater than a "happy meal" and an overstuffed belly.

A few minutes after this small group exited the building, their waiter came, almost frantically, out of the restaurant. The group could immediately tell he was looking for something. His eyes systematically began scanning the parking lot. As they locked onto what had surely been his favorite table of the day, his expression immediately turned to one of relief. As soon as he spotted who he was looking for, he walked over to the group, thanking them profusely and shaking their hands with great vigor.

"We were glad to bless you," someone from the small group said with a smile, expecting that this would be the end of the conversation.

"You don't understand how much this means to me," the waiter began to say as he immediately broke into tears.

For the next few moments, between his sobbing, the man explained that his family was supposed to move to Georgia in the next few days. Due to some financial setbacks and the overwhelming scope of the cost of moving, however, the family didn't have enough to complete the move. The deadline to leave was just days away, but they didn't have what they needed to make the journey. They would have to leave their current place of residence, but didn't have enough provision to get to the next.

In order to make up for the shortfall, this family man had left the task of completing the packing and preparations to his wife and children while he picked up every single shift he could beg the management and other waiters to give him. Since this location was a 24-hour restaurant, this often included both very late and very early hours. He was doing everything he could to make enough to provide for his family. At roughly $2 to $4 a table, he planned to work every hour he was physically able for those last few days.

Through tears, the man repeated, "You may never understand just how much this means to me." As the tears spread from the waiter to the rest of the group, someone asked if they could pray for the server and his family in this season of transition.

"I'd like that very much," he said as these new friends let their tear soaked words fall gently into the hands of the One who did not come to be served, but to show His children the power and joy that is only discovered in the heart of a servant.

[For Personal Growth]

Find a way to serve someone else every single day this week. It doesn't have to be "big." Just serve someone.

[With A Group]

Share with the group the worst experience you ever had at a restaurant. What made this experience so unfavorably memorable?

As a group, read and discuss Mark 10:35-45.

What surprises you? What challenges you? What are you noticing for the first time? What stands out to you?

How does serving others make us more like Jesus?

When was the last time you served someone?

How would your life (and the lives of those around you) forever change if you took on the attitude of a servant?

If there is time, share and discuss anything else from this chapter that challenged you.

Before you close in prayer, discuss as a group how you can serve together in your church and/or in your community.

Pick a person (or a couple people) to organize the event, remind people when and where to show up, and what to bring.

[Our Serving Opportunity]

[FOURTEEN]

GOD vs THE INTERGALACTIC SEESAW
We Can Play On It On Our Way To The Restaurant At The End Of The Universe

> "You are a breathtaking reflection of God's heart for me.
> How He pursued me, and loved me, even when I did not
> love myself. You held my hand in the darkness,
> and you pulled me out into the light."
> **Tyler Perry, From _Madea's Family Reunion_**

I grew up in Wyoming. I may have mentioned that. As the single least populous state in the union, it is a statistical truth that relatively few people are able to make this exact claim. This makes meeting someone from Wyoming like finding Bigfoot or discovering a special breed of unicorn with a rare golden horn. Most people will never in their life truly experience Wyoming. That is, they will never experience Wyoming _outside of_ the tourist traps like Jackson Hole, Devil's Tower, or Old Faithful in Yellowstone.

Since many will never truly encounter the arctic tundra that is Wyoming, there are a few things in need of explanation. First of all, Wyoming has four seasons, like everyone else. They just have four _different_ seasons than everyone else. The seasons in Wyoming are as follows: winter, still winter, two-months-of-warmth, and almost winter again. There is no "fall." There is not really a "spring." It's snow... lots and lots of snow.

You may think I am exaggerating, but I have literally watched 4th of July fireworks while wearing a jacket and marveling as the explosions in the sky burst through small flurries of white flakes. Sure, that wasn't every year, but the fact that it even happened once, in retrospect, amazes me. Most people across the country are thinking about how to make their kids "cute" or "scary" around Halloween each year. In Wyoming the highest priority is to properly insulate your kids costume so they don't freeze to literal death. I'm not making that up.

Some native Wyomingites would argue for different seasons than what I have mentioned above. Hunting season, for example, is a highly popular season, perhaps deserving of its own designation on the official Wyoming calendar. During hunting season, churches and businesses alike struggle to maintain even 3/4 their usual flow of people or customers. However, since it mostly happens across late two-months-of-warmth and almost winter again, I feel I can group that one into my original designations.

It does seem that, like other parts of the globe, the climate has shifted quite a bit in the two-plus decades since I have actually lived in Wyoming. That being said, I have rather recent pictures on my iCloud photo storage of what other states call "fall" where everything is so completely covered by snow that it is like trying to play "Where's Waldo" to spot my mother's car outside. I also have a very neat picture from just a few years ago where the heads of the screws on the inside of the outside door handle on my mother's house were so frozen solid that they had literally turned white with frostbite. So, while some may argue that Wyoming is no longer, or perhaps never was, a tundra, I have photographic evidence that begs to differ.

Just as the predominant theme of the seasons in Wyoming is "cold," the dominant status of the air around that part of the country is "wind." Were Captain Planet and the Planeteers to come and visit Wyoming, they would not need the girl with the wind ring at all. She would just have to sit around, because her job would be done for her by nature itself.

Have you ever seen a tumbleweed in your entire lifetime? Maybe that one time you visited grandpa and grandma at their farm? I have seen a literal migration of them... recently. I have witnessed a tumbleweed the size of a small Volkswagen. Chicago may be the "Windy City," but Wyoming takes that mantle when it comes to being the "Windy State."

When you live in such a cold and windy place for more than a few rotations of the seasons, you learn stuff. For example, one year, while I was in Grade School, mom decided that we needed to plant some trees in the front yard of our new house. Someday, she reasoned, these trees will be mighty sources of wood that anchor the front of the grassy kingdom known as our front yard. In that moment, however, they looked like twigs.

That day, we dug a somewhat deep hole in the yard, carefully placed the sapling into the ground, then used the dirt we had dug up to fill in the space again. In that moment I thought "job well done." However, as I started to walk away I heard a prompting voice say, "And just where do you think you're going?"

As it turns out, when you're done planting a tree in Wyoming, you're only half way done with the process of planting a tree in Wyoming. My mother then went to the nearby garage and grabbed four long green spikes that had regular protrusions, some rope, some old dish cloths, and an oversized hammer.

"Here," she said as I looked at her in confusion.

"Mom, I'm not sure what sort of science experiment we're about to undergo, but I'm pretty sure its the combination of the dish cloth and clown hammer that's getting me here."

I was about to learn a lesson that would later take on a much more profound meaning. You see, Wyoming is windy. No, I mean it is really windy. Perhaps you've seen jokes floating around the internet about "Wyoming windsocks." A windsock is a conical shaped piece of fabric that is attached to a pole. As wind flows through it, it will either rise, flap, or completely fill with air. At one point in history, apparently, people used these to "measure" how much wind was out that day. The joke is that people in Wyoming simply put old rusty chains on poles. Where it stops being funny is how those chains often are blowing at full mast, as if they were mere fabric.

As a tree grows, these strong winds consistently push against the sapling, causing it to grow with an unhealthy leaning towards one direction or the other. Should this happen, your options are to live with a crooked and twisting tree in front of your house and risk only having a few brave visitors when it comes time to trick-or-treat, or to make a nice warm fire in the fireplace and start over. Because of the strong winds, trees simply cannot be planted and then left to their own natural course of growing. If additional steps are not taken, the tree is likely to grow malformed and may even die.

When planting a tree, you must also plant up to 4 long stakes that stand opposite one another. Once you have hammered these deeply into the ground with your clown hammer or mallet, you must then take a piece of rope and make a loop, placing the tree in one end of the loop with the loose ends tied around a post. You should also put an old dish cloth between the rope and the tree, so the rope doesn't sink down into the tree over time. From there, you must systematically tighten the ropes at each post until each one is pulling on the tree, lightly but firmly trying to make it come in that direction.

It is only when all four (or so) posts are equally pulling on the tree that the tree is safe. While it likely doesn't feel comfortable to the tree to be tugged in four different opposing directions at once, the time it spends growing in the tension of these forces will ensure the tree is able to grow straight and strong.

This is a parallel to life itself. We all need proper and healthy tension to grow and mature in our spirits and in our hearts. This theme shows up quite a few times in Scripture. In Ephesians chapter 4, after explaining the role of pastors to be those who equip followers of Jesus to do the work of ministry, we see this:

> "... until we all reach unity in the faith and in the knowledge of God's Son, growing into maturity with a stature measured by Christ's fullness. Then we will no longer be little children, tossed by the waves and blown around by every wind of teaching, by human cunning with cleverness in the techniques of deceit. But speaking the truth in love, let us grow in every way into Him who is the head - Christ" (Ephesians 4:13-16 NLT).

Notice how this pregnant verse speaks of "growing into maturity" and how we are compared to something small that is growing up towards something much larger. This verse shows us that we need some tension in our faith if we are to grow into the fullness of Christ without being "tossed by the waves and blown around by every wind of teaching."

Perhaps this is why the Christian faith is so full of paradoxes. It is hard to read very far in Scripture without encountering both/and realities that shouldn't be reduced to either/or choices. It is the tensions in our faith journey and a healthy questioning of our theology that helps our faith grow strong and straight.

In the previous chapter we talked about a few of these paradoxes of the upside-down Kingdom. We encountered several of these both/and realities that should not be reduced to either/or choices, such as "the last shall become first," and "the one who wants to be great should serve." As Ephesians 4 points out, our world does all it can to reduce these paradoxes to either/or. The world tries to get us to go all in on one and all out on the other.

The world tells us that if you want to be great, focus on yourself. "Just do you." "Take care of number one." "Don't trust anyone." "Don't take *bat guano* from anyone." On and on and on it goes. We are blown by strong winds of human teaching in one direction. If our faith is not held in tension, we grow bent and broken, leaning one way, or worse, teeter-tottering between opposing ideas.

Reggie Joiner, founder of ReThink and Orange, regularly tours the church world and talks about these tensions. As he speaks, he pulls out a rubber band and places one end on a nail before stretching the rubber across to another nail. As the rubber connects with each post, it is held in tension. Reggie will often pluck the rubber band to show that it now has power stored up in it. He'll then flop around another rubber band to show how the one without any tension coursing through it also lacks any real power.

It is from this illustration that Reggie begins talking about some of the tensions we face in our Christian faith. Tensions such as the reality that we can KNOW God, but God is also a MYSTERY. We can be transformed in a MOMENT, but it takes FOREVER to figure out what that means. The BIBLE is all true, but not everything that is true about LIFE is found in the Bible. TRUST leads to a stronger faith, however DOUBT also makes our faith stronger. Our BELIEFS should matter to us, and they certainly matter to God, but PEOPLE also matter[32].

Perhaps my favorite that Joiner shares is that God does indeed have a standard or IDEAL, but God also chooses to use BROKEN people. I would argue that broken people are God's instrument of choice, yet there is still such a thing as damning sin and its consequences. All of these things are true, yet they create a tension inside of us. They are paradoxes. They are both/and realities that should not be reduced to either/or choices.

The trap that "human understanding" and the enemy of our souls try to lay out for us is to remove the tension. Satan wants nothing more than for us to go all right or all left. The devil knows that, like the rubber band, we are powerless when tension is removed. If he can get us to go far left, nothing will be right. If he can get us to go far to the right, nothing will be left. Best of all, if he can get us to blow back and forth across our lifetime between two opinions, he's got us exactly where he wants us.

If we go all in on the idea that we must forcibly and blindly trust God, our faith will crash when we doubt. If we live purely in doubt, without life-saving trust, we will never give our heart to God. If we go all in on the idea that God is purely a mystery, we will have no concrete faith to ground us, yet if we dive deeply into the idea that we can somehow know everything about God and leave no room for mystery, we soon create a god in our own image that is small enough to fit inside our brains.

If we focus on the moment of salvation only, we will forever chase that mountaintop experience. Then, when life isn't immediately roses and bubble baths, we will quickly abandon the joy of our first love. Yet, if we focus purely on the ongoing journey and forget that everything can change in a moment, our faith will be as dry and dusty as the long roads we force our bleeding feet to trudge.

Do you see how important holding our faith in tension is? This isn't to say that nothing is all-true. This doesn't mean we make God half of everything and fully nothing. It means we must hold those things that are whole yet seemingly different in tension and allow God to work even when we can't wrap our mind fully around Him. It is by living and growing in the tension that we no longer act like spiritual infants, but live in the fullness of Christ.

The problem is that instead of holding our faith in tension like a rubber band ready to fly, we treat our faith like a seesaw. Perhaps you remember this piece of playground equipment from your childhood. The idea of a seesaw is simple, it's a plank on a pivot. When you push down on one side, the other rises.

I still have nightmares about these things from when I was a kid. I may have mentioned, but I was a little heavier than my classmates. When everyone else was packing 50 to 70 pounds, I had already hit just over 100 pounds. That may not sound like much of a difference, but when I sat on the seesaw, my friends shot up into the air and didn't come back down. This was rather embarrassing, so it didn't take me long to abandon that unholy contraption entirely.

Unfortunately, instead of leaving the seesaw in the playground of our infant faith where it belongs, many of us play on it long into old age and apparent "spiritual maturity." Rather than holding our faith in the tensions that God so clearly provides, we falsely split apart Godly paradoxes and place them on either side of the intergalactic seesaw. When we find evidence supporting one side or the other, we go push down on that side and watch as the other side flies high.

This is always happening in society, as well. We place ideas that should live in tension on opposite sides of the seesaw every generation or two. Take patriotism, as a very quick example. I grew up in the 1980's when it was popular to be patriotic. American flags proudly adorned people's clothing and their American-made cars. You could immediately tell who the hero in the movie (or wrestling ring) was by the depth of their allegiance to the flag, anthem, and the American Bald Eagle. Likewise, you could immediately tell who the enemy in the movie was just by measuring the twang of their accent.

In the 80's we listened to *America, The Beautiful, God Bless America,* and (especially for those who grew up with Hulk Hogan as the ultimate good guy) *Real American*. Everything Americana was great and anything foreign, especially in the world of cars, was garbage. If we picture this aspect of culture as one end of the seesaw, then, in my lifetime it was at its highest point in the 1980's. Then the 1990's happened.

No sooner had Kurt Cobain chain-smoked his way onto the scene than the seesaw traded sides. Increasingly, the theme was now *DIS*trust in America. The "Real American Hero" of the 80's was replaced by the untrusting anti-hero of the 90's and early 00's. It was during this time that our news highlighted government corruption, political lies, overcrowded prisons, gang violence, and more. As the world became more connected, our 80's patriotism suddenly began to look more and more like xenophobia.

American movie goers became increasingly unsettled when the straight Protestant middle-class white guy was shown as the hero and the person of ethnic descent was portrayed as the enemy. The bad guy was more and more likely to end up being the untrustworthy rich white guy, who was only ever really in it for the money, while the protagonists took on more ethnic identities and backgrounds.

Songs in this era lamented "I'm afraid of Americans" (Trent Reznor and David Bowie) and "America, please come back to me baby" (Sonny Sandoval and Carlos Santana). T-shirts encouraged us once again to not trust anyone. Movies like *Enemy of the State* and *Eagle Eye* showed the protagonist running from a corrupt government that was always all around us, controlling and recording our every move.

Then 9/11 (2001) happened. Overnight, the seesaw changed sides once again. Suddenly, crosses were being worn around people's necks and the American flag waived proudly from every porch. Foreigners were once again untrustworthy characters. Being "American" became a key part of people's identities as it had decades earlier.

A cursory look across the last 100 years of history will definitively show the seesaw rise and fall, almost predictably. Though it is a little too simplistic, we often characterize these rises and falls by decades. Just ask yourself what comes to mind when you picture (or remember) the 1950's. Apple pie and America, right? Everyone holding to a strict moral code.

Yet, the force of the 50's also pushed the next generation, roughly the 1960's, to rebel against all of that. The 60's replaced good citizenry and a strict moral code with free love and a rejection of "the man's" rules. The children of the 70's rebelled against their parents. The 80's rad kids rebelled against their parents, ironically by becoming conservatives… and so on. Roughly every ten to fifteen years the intergalactic seesaw would switch sides. Not liking the world around you right now? It is likely that the seesaw is not far from pushing off again.

As long as the devil can keep us on the seesaw, no matter which extreme we adopt, he has won. We either go right where nothing is left, or we go left where nothing is right. Either way, Satan laughs as the seesaw goes up on one end and down on the other. He has us. We're "blown about" and, like an un-stretched rubber band, we have no power. This is why Scripture frequently points to a paradoxical and unexpected different way.

When asked whether or not it was lawful to pay taxes, Jesus didn't fall into a political argument. Instead, He went a paradoxical and unexpected different way that embraced the tension. When confronted with religious legalism that said people shouldn't be healed on the Sabbath, as religious leaders were wondering if Jesus was going to break or uphold the Jewish law, Jesus went a paradoxical and unexpected different way that embraced the tension. God did this frequently in Old Testament times, and Jesus taught a Master's-level class in it.

We fall into this seesaw trap more often than we would care to admit. This is why some are confident that they can know God and leave no room for mystery. My favorite example of this is founding father Thomas Jefferson. While it is debatable to what degree any of the founding fathers actually held to an authentic faith in Jesus, as many were more truly Deists, Jefferson's story lives in the realm of the fantastic.

Perhaps you have seen *The Jefferson Bible* before. Do you know why there is a version of the Bible attributed to Thomas Jefferson? It is because Jefferson's dominant place on the seesaw was that everything could and should be known or knowable. Jefferson had no place for miracles or mysteries in life. He had no room for the fantastic or the spiritual. Yet, like most others in that historical timeframe, Jefferson was expected to read the Bible.

The problem Jefferson faced is that the Bible is FULL of paradoxical tension when it comes to what is natural and what is actually supernatural. The Bible shows a powerful adherence to science, almost as if the same Being that created the "known" universe also had a hand in the creation of holy Scripture (wink wink). However, Scripture also shows that our natural realm may not actually be the most true reality that surrounds us and points to a Spiritual realm that impacts our natural order.

Jefferson would have none of this tension. It just didn't fit his side of the intergalactic seesaw. So, what did our founding father do? Long before the sort of software that allows me to direct my words at your brain through the medium of pixels on a screen, Jefferson went old-school (would it just have been called "school" then?) and scrapbooked himself a Bible that fit his side of the seesaw. Jefferson literally cut out any part of the Bible he didn't like or agree with, especially anything that had to do with miracles or a spiritual realm beyond our physical touch. What remained was a sanitized "version" of the Bible that could rest comfortably on Jefferson's side of the seesaw without moving it even one subscripted iota back towards the other side.

Before we throw rocks at little Tommy from our spot on the playground, it would do us well to admit that we're all guilty of this in one way or another. Perhaps that is why the book of Revelation warns of the consequences one will face should someone remove or add anything to it. As imperfect followers of Jesus, we often put heavier weights on one side of the seesaw or the other. Just like Thomas Jefferson, we often cut and paste Scripture into our preferred version of the Bible and increasingly ignore anything that might push the seesaw.

What if Jesus is wanting us to go in a paradoxical and unexpected different way?

What are some areas of the faith that you have failed to hold in tension? Does it scare you to think you might have to come down from your side of the seesaw? Does it unsettle you that the seesaw itself is an Admiral Ackbar meme-level trap from the beginning?

The thought of getting off the seesaw scares us, even if we come to understand its diabolical nature. Seesaws are easier to play on, after all. It's binary. There's just up or down. It's not as complicated as the tension that exists in a game like Marco Polo, where you are forced to test the very nature of reality and your perception of it regularly. Seesaws are uncomplicated. They don't force us to live in healthy tension.

Yet, we must learn to live in the tension a little more if we're to become like Jesus. After all, if there was anyone who lived in this fullness, it was Jesus. Scripture shows us that He was both fully man and fully God. He was two distinct sets of 100% at the same time. He wasn't sometimes more God than man (as the seesaw was falling more to one side than the other), nor was He sometimes more man than God. He was both, fully, in every moment, without wavering.

As fully God, Jesus was sinless. In fact, despite what your drunk friends might claim about themselves, Jesus was the only sinless person to ever live. He was the best there was, the best there is, and the best there ever will be. Yet, in His sinless perfection, Jesus often hung around notoriously broken sinners. What's up with that? That doesn't fit on one side of the seesaw. That creates tension.

Even Jesus' public proclamations lived in the tension. He told the world that the Kingdom of God/Heaven was at hand, but then also told us it was not yet. Which is it? Yes. It isn't either/or, it was, is, and until the Second Coming will be both/and. Jesus was always talking like this. If you want to find true life, die to yourself. If you try to save your life, you'll lose it. It's just so upside-down. Then again, since Jesus created everything, I guess we're once again the ones who are hanging from our seesaws that we've bolted to the ceiling.

We need to wrestle with healthy tension in so many areas of our faith. Perhaps you need to take a moment and think through how you have been jumping up and down on the seesaw instead of discovering the power that comes from being held in perfect tension. For those who are ready for it, we are about to examine one powerful tension in Scripture that will help us better understand the nature and character of God.

Sorry Mr. Jefferson, but we need to dive into a deep mystery that lives on every page of Scripture. We need to examine one place where we often get trapped on the seesaw when it comes to understanding God. We need to examine a tension that has the ability to rewrite our very understanding of the molecules that compose our brains and the electrical impulses we consider to be thoughts. It's time to get off the seesaw and move onward into unmapped terrain.

[For Personal Growth]

What aspects of your life or faith are straightforward and simple truth?

How do you know these things to be true?

What are some areas of your life, faith, or identity that seem to be sitting on one side of the seesaw or the other?

In what ways is Jesus calling you to take an unexpected different way when it comes to these tensions?

[With A Group]

Continue reading the next chapter before discussing both chapters as a group.

[My Next Step]

[FIFTEEN]

GOD AS HOLY LOVE

All You Need is (Holy) Love, Love. (Holy) Love is All You Need.

"Trade love for the city lights. You chose me to stay.
Trade light for the city of love. You chose me to stay."
Blindside, "City Lights"

Over the course of my undergraduate years, studying to become a pastor, I interned in five different churches in five different parts of the country. I spent one summer sweltering in the humid sauna of Lake Charles, Louisiana. I did two internships in different parts of Kentucky, where I learned about Ale-8 and marathon sessions of the game foursquare. I interned with a massive church in Oklahoma City, and I even got to spend a summer as a youth intern at my home church in Casper, Wyoming.

Prior to that, I spent nine months of my life training as a professional wrestler with the Christian Wrestling Federation in Rockwall, Texas. In the years since, I spent just over a decade living in Moore, Oklahoma, and a few years in Columbus, Ohio. Then, just about two years ago, God led us to what we feel and pray will be an *incredibly* lengthy season of life spent in the shadow of the Rocky Mountains in Denver, Colorado.

Having spent some not insignificant amounts of time in such varied parts of the country, I have come to learn a few things about how the intergalactic seesaw is played upon in differing regions. Let's take, for example, a key distinction I learned between the Northwestern and Mid-South part of the USA when compared to the American Midwest. Well, I should clarify that though people in Ohio say they are in the "Midwest," if you were to draw a line down the middle of the North American continent, they would clearly be the Mid-East, but that logic doesn't seem to play well in the Buckeye state. I digress.

The difference in where each region sits on the seesaw became screamingly clear when we moved to Ohio. Having spent 10+ years in Oklahoma (20+ years for my wife), there were a few things about "what all Christians should just know" that came into sudden contrast. In the Mid-South, it is understood that if you drink alcohol, you probably really aren't a Christian, and if you don't know how to handle a gun, you likely don't *really* know Jesus.

These rules somehow didn't make it to Ohio. Two events in particular caught me off guard and almost knocked me off of my place on the seesaw. The first was more innocuous. It would have been easy to miss. Upon moving from the place "where the wind goes sweeping down the plains" to O-H-I-O, my wife and I were at the home of some of the leadership of our new church. Within moments of getting settled in, someone asked "Pastor, can I get you a beer or anything?" "Renae, would you like a glass of wine?"

The church leader who offered had no idea that my wife and I had spent the majority of our lives being told that Christians, especially pastors, were not allowed to consume alcohol. Yet, it was offered so casually here that they were almost shocked when we declined. It did not take us long to figure out through several similar instances that we were considered a little odd for not partaking.

The second incident was more obvious and comical. During a weekly staff gathering, I was sharing about a pastor friend of mine in Kansas named Danny. It is important to the story to understand that Danny REALLY loves Jesus. You don't get too far into any conversation before Danny has brought Him up. Danny also really loves hunting, shooting guns, owning guns, trading guns, talking about guns, and stockpiling guns as if he were a one-man militia. If the zombie apocalypse ever became a thing, you can bet my wife and I's very first move would be to track down Danny. He would survive it.

In fact, one time while I was visiting Danny in Kansas, we were driving along a road that was predictably encapsulated on all sides by open farmland when Danny excitedly shouted something like, "There's that varmint." What happened next was part blur and part James Bond movie. Danny cranked the steering wheel and slammed the brakes so that the vehicle was instantly pointing the other direction. Within the expanse of a split second, Danny had produced a gun, Lord knows from where, had rolled down his window (mid-Tokyo drift!?!), and was unloading lead into the open field.

As my jaw finally rolled back up to meet my upper row of teeth, I asked Danny what had just happened.

"I saw that dang coyote (pronounced k-eye-yoat) that's been bothering our chickens running across that field." Yep. That is exactly what I remember him saying. Those very words.

In my confusion and rushing adrenaline I couldn't think of a better question to utter than, "Did you get him?"

"Na, just missed him." Danny calmly, yet dejectedly, proclaimed as he turned the vehicle back towards our original destination with a sudden return to all proper traffic ettiequte.

As I told this story to a group of seven pastors and five or six support staff, I could see that they weren't as amused by this occurrence as I clearly was. For a moment, no one really said anything. Finally, one of the pastors broke the silence.

"… and this guy is a pastor?"

"Yeah. He is the senior pastor of…"

"And, yet… he owns gunSSSS?" The s's were clearly emphasized to point out that there was an element of surprise other than the James Bond goes John Deere side of the story.

"Yeah… he has a few dozen of them, I would bet."

I continued to get wide-eyed stares.

"And, you're sure he's a pastor?" Someone sheepishly asked again.

145

A few weeks later, as I was speaking at a youth camp, I came across a church that was offering concealed carry classes. They noted this fact on their church sign that sat prominently in the front yard. Their next-door neighbors, who obviously (in their eyes) knew better, had purchased a near-identical sign. On their sign, they had simply put the words "this church is an abomination to the Lord."

What I came to discover is that in the Northerly Mid-East part of the country, it is just understood that if you own a gun, you probably aren't really a Christian, and if you don't drink alcohol, you may not actually know Jesus. This is that region's preferred place on the seesaw.

I used American patriotism as my example of choice in the last chapter to illustrate the fact that our society has been pushing the seesaw up and down for as long as any one of us has been alive. Just as our strict adherence to the Red, White, and Blue has risen to points where we cry over the anthem, and fallen to points where to be considered "pure-blooded American patriotic" is an affront to Native Americans and other countries, so too has one of the core tensions that exists within our theology of God risen and fallen across generations.

In case you're wondering, this core element of our theology is not whether Jesus would own a gun or whether or not He would drink "actual alcohol," as opposed to grape juice communion. It is something so much more important than that. Yet, this misunderstanding of God is so ingrained in us based upon which generational point in history we happen to occupy and which region of the country is currently governing our thoughts, that we may have missed it entirely.

Perhaps the single biggest aspect of our theology that must be held in proper and delicate tension, but instead gets shoehorned onto the intergalactic seesaw, is that of God's love "verses" His holiness. These should-be-complementary aspects of His nature are divided away from the character of God and then used to divide humanity into polarizing opinions and dangerous beliefs. What is meant to be a both/and reality in our understanding of God has been reduced to either/or arguments which are violently held.

Let's take a look, for example, at two important pieces of God's Word. "The one who does not love does not know God, because God is love" (1 John 4:8 CSB). "Each of the four living creatures had six wings; they were covered with eyes around and inside. Day and night they never stop saying, 'Holy, holy, holy, Lord God, the Almighty, who was, who is, and who is to come" (Revelation 4:8 CSB).

In these two pieces of God's Word, both conveniently denoted with chapter four, verse eight in their respective book, we see what the world around us has used to trap us into a seesaw position more than perhaps any other aspect of theology. In fact, if you watch the teeter-totter rise and fall across the generations, you can begin to see just how problematic we have made these two ideas; God is love. God is holy.

When I was younger, the side of the intergalactic theological seesaw being most heavily sat upon was the holiness of God. It was simply understood that followers of Jesus didn't drink, smoke, cuss, chew, or go with girls who do. It was simply understood that followers of Jesus didn't attend R-rated movies (unless, for some reason that movie was titled *Braveheart* or *Gladiator*, as those somehow made it into sermon illustrations frequently). It was simply understood that there were rules that were meant to be followed.

If someone was caught living "below the standard," then we should have nothing to do with such a person and, perhaps, that person deserved the ire we sent their way as we actively shunned said persons. This attitude gave rise to the term "holy rollers." Those "holier than thou" people who lived up to a standard that they expected every other human to understand by osmosis or risk the Luigi death stare.

As Church of God (Anderson, IN) scholar Merle Strege notes,

> "In the nineteenth century, American holiness preachers interpreted (John) Wesley's doctrine of Christian perfection to emphasize avoidance of 'wordliness...' A 'holy and blameless' life was often described in negative terms. Thus, true Christians didn't frequent forms of entertainment like dances, theaters, or ballgames. They didn't wear neckties or hats with feathers, and pleats were not found in their dresses. Nor did Christians use tobacco in any form, or drink alcoholic beverages, coffee, or tea. Accordingly, one Church of God saint testified that she was 'saved and sanctified from all forms of hot drinks[33].'"

Scripture regularly speaks of a God who is holy and calls us to a standard. P. T. Forsyth once noted that "everything begins and ends in our Christian theology with the holiness of God[34]." Simon Ponsonby, Pastor of Theology at St. Aldates Church of Oxford, England adds, "take the notion of holiness out of Christianity, and you have nothing much left to say, be, or do[35]."

The word "holy" means "set apart." This "set apart-ed-ness" becomes a part of our story from the very beginning of all creation. The first five words in the Bible are "in the beginning, God created…" This immediately shows us a Being which is separated from the entirety of all that is created, for this Being is, in fact, the Creator.

Just as what truly constitutes me as a soul-filled human being cannot be contained fully within the words that I now write, so too God, as Creator, cannot be limited to that which we see in His creation. While the words on the page reflect my thoughts, they are two dimensional and flat, where as I am three-dimensional and, depending on my strict adherence to my calorie counting app, rather roundish.

In similar fashion, all of creation, even in its multidimensional glory, is a pale comparison to the "beyond-ness" of God. He is "set apart" from creation and is far greater than the sum of all the molecules of the universe from expanse to expanse combined and multiplied by infinity. Not only is God holy and set apart, but He calls us to be set apart, as well.

> "Therefore, with your minds ready for action, be sober-minded and set your hope completely on the grace to be brought to you at the revelation of Jesus Christ. As children, do not be conformed to the desires of your former ignorance. But as the one who called you is holy, you are also to be holy in all your conduct; for it is written 'be holy, because I am holy' (1 Peter 1:13-16 CSB).

As mentioned, the holiness of God, as it has been expressed in societal norms, has primarily been about external expressions. It has just been understood throughout the past decades that "decent people" didn't do certain things. This often meant that "normal, good, kind people" didn't get tattoos, use foul language, or listen to certain types of music. Further, those who were self-decidedly "holy" and "above" would often look down upon those who were "lesser" because of their life choices.

Thinking in our global society has changed dramatically over the past couple decades, however. Just as a pendulum hits its highest point before dramatically reversing its momentum towards the opposite spectrum, society has shifted its focus from "right living" to whatever it is in this moment that we define as "love." To say that "love" is the current and dominant position on the intergalactic seesaw would be quite an understatement. It would be foolhardy to try to argue otherwise.

As I transcribe these pixels onto a screen, while sitting in a Starbucks in Denver, Colorado, I am not far from a local church who has added an enormous banner to the side of their building that includes the words "love is love." As I type these words on my screen hoping that they might one day find themselves as pixels invading the optic canal of others, two of our country's greatest musical superstars have just released an album entitled *Everything is Love*.

Just as Scripture is clear that God is holy, stating it three times in sequence for emphasis, so too the Holy Bible is clear that love isn't just something nice that God has to offer. God does not simply provide love. God **is** love. Love is an irreducible aspect of God's makeup and His character.

There is no **true** love apart from God, for love flows from God as its only source. All "love" that we as humans share is nothing but borrowed capitol from the character of God. Apart from the love that is God, we are unable to love anything at all. That statement is bold, I understand, but it is as Scripture affirms, we love God because He first loved us (1 John 4:19). God is "patient zero" when it comes to "the love bug."

The problem with our current societal view of love is exactly that we have come to believe "everything is love." We dare not tell someone that what they believe, or are experiencing, isn't really love. Even our usage of the term "love is love" causes the term to lose a definable meaning. Saying "love is love" is like saying "that rock is a rock." However true the words are that come out of your mouth, you haven't yet said anything of consequence. What kind of rock is it?

When holiness reigned the playground, many felt that the strict adherence to rules had gone too far. Children who could not live up to their parent's definition of "the right standard" might literally be cast out of the family. Friends who did not live up to "what is right" would become outcasts from the group. The holiness of the holy rollers caused harm to many.

While some would proclaim that they were being "a little harsh" for the person's own good and that it was to help them grow, this course of action rarely lead to repentance. I'm not sure it ever could have, as

Scripture affirms boldly that it is the kindness of God that leads us to repentance (Romans 2:4). And, those words were written by a Pharisee! They were the religious leaders who lived and died, and killed others, due to a strict adherence to the holy law.

Love and holiness have battled throughout history to have the dominant place on the intergalactic seesaw. If the pattern of this world is to be believed, love and holiness are something akin to pre-existent opposites battling for the hearts and minds of humanity from the moment the first human cell came into existence. But, remember, the seesaw itself is a trap.

Love and holiness were *never* on opposite sides.

God is not either holy or loving. Both are irreducible aspects of the nature and character of God. The problem is, our soda can minds are often too small to contain such powerful tension. Even those who recognize the need for this healthy tension often get it wrong. This is why we do everything we can to redefine sin to fit the personal preferences of those around us so as not to offend anyone while also holding to "our convictions." This is watered down, middle of the road, neither hot nor cold, time to get spit from God's mouth territory.

We simply don't know how to get off of the seesaw.

The reality is that God is paradoxically BOTH holy AND love. The two are not opposites, they may, in fact, be varied expressions of the same thing. If anyone understood this, it was a disciple named John. John was referred to as "the disciple Jesus loved," and yet He frequently wrote about God being "light;" Light that is pure, holy, without blemish.

John is the one who, as we looked at above, noted that God **is** love. As the late night infomercial would say, "but wait, there's more." John is also the recipient of, and author of, the revelation of Jesus the Christ that is recorded in the writing bearing the name *Revelation*. John didn't allow us to see God as either love or holy. John's witness of Jesus powerfully proclaims that both are found only and at their truest in Him.

While we can see the both/and reality of God's holy love throughout every page of Scripture, John is a good place to start. John writes in the opening chapter of his gospel account of the life of Jesus the Christ that, "The Word became flesh and dwelt among us. We observed His glory, the glory as the one and only Son, from the Father, **full** of grace and truth" (John 1:14 CSB, emphasis added).

When trying to reconcile the both/and reality of God's nature as holy, holy, holy love, we often see Him as half full. He is half full of holiness and half full of love. When these combustive elements are combined in a cosmic beaker, we see the fullness of God. This, however is a deadly misconception from the very beginning.

Few honest theologians would argue that God is NOT love or NOT holy. They would simply argue over how much holiness and exactly what measurement of love has gone into the mixture and whether or not that is in line with the original recipe. In order to reconcile their particular seat on the seesaw they do their best to attempt to hold it perfectly balanced in the middle.

As He often does, however, Jesus shows us that there is a paradoxical and unexpected different way. John tells us that "the Word," a Socratic reference to Jesus Himself, was **full** of both. He is not half full of love and half full of holiness. God is fully love. God is fully holy. The recipe calls for two 100%s. So, how do we understand this seeming paradox. How can something be 100% comprised of two things?

Once again, we turn to Jesus. The paradox that Jesus was fully God and fully man is furthered by the paradox that Jesus is the full and perfect embodiment of real love and real holiness. This is exemplified, among other places, in John chapter 8. Here we see a woman who was caught in the physical act of adultery by some real old-school (again, just "school" that far back?) holy-rollers. These religious leaders see their opportunity and they use this woman to trap Jesus.

The Law (holiness code) of God notes that such persons would have to be stoned to death for their crime, yet Jesus had been on tour showing God's love through healings and moments of unexpected and unreasonable forgiveness. In effect, these religious leaders were attempting to put Jesus into a Kobayashi Maru.

Do you remember the J. J. Abrams reboot of Gene Rodenberry's *Star Trek*? In this 2009 film, Captain James Tiberius Kirk is presented with a situation that is intentionally unbeatable. The system is designed against him to provide no other outcome but humiliating defeat. This is exactly the sort of scenario that the religious leaders were attempting to place Jesus in. If Jesus lets this woman off the hook, He would be guilty of transgression of the holy Law of God. If, however, He allowed her to be stoned, He would be going against the unreasonable love and forgiveness He had so frequently displayed.

These religious leaders had placed Jesus into an unbeatable scenario. They had forced Him to face the Kobayashi Maru. However, like Kirk does in the movie, Jesus goes in an unexpected different way. Jesus does not reject either the holiness of God, nor the love of God. Instead, He unexpectedly fully embodies them both. Not half of either, but fully both.

As discussed in an earlier chapter, Jesus tells the crowd that the one who is without sin should throw the first stone. In other words, He had first right of refusal. Jesus was the only one without sin, and this group seems to have known it. One by one, they all walk away. I resonate more and more with the text as it notes that the order of departure was from oldest to youngest. The older I get, the more clearly I see my own faults, failures, and need for a Savior.

Soon enough, only Jesus and this woman remained. After what must have felt like an excruciatingly long time to this woman, whose life was quite literally in Jesus' hands in that moment, He spoke to her. In the midst of this paradoxical moment, Jesus did something wholly unexpected. He forgave her.

If you read back Jesus' words, "He who is without sin should cast the first stone;" that meant that only Jesus had the right to throw rocks. Yet, He excused her. However, you can't see the fullness of this moment unless you see what happened next. He didn't just forgive her in His love, He upheld a holy standard as He told her to "go and sin no longer." It was not either/or, it was both/and.

Jesus isn't half full of two incongruent forces, He is perfectly full of holy love. Holiness, if it is truly the weight of that which is holy, is full of love. Love, if it truly love at all, is fully holy. There is no separation of the two. Jesus was "full" of grace and truth. As Juli Slattery has pointed out, "As we study His life, He never compromised truth in order to love people well. And, He never compromised love in order to honor God's truth well[36]."

Emphasizing God's love at the expense of His holiness gives us an incapable god who would never call us to do anything difficult and would be aghast to call our personal choices "sin." Emphasizing God's holiness at the expense of His love gives us a caricature of God who is filled with misplaced wrath and cruel judgment. God is not either holy or loving. He is not either loving or holy. God's holiness and love are not exclusive from one another. They simply cannot be separated.

My apologies to Beyonce and Jay-Z for their confusion, but if "everything is love" then absolutely nothing is. If everything is love, then rape is love. If everything is love, then racism is love. If everything is love, then sex trafficking is love. If everything is love, then hatred is love and all love is actually hatred. Yes, love is love... but only when we understand that love and holiness cannot be separated, even on a molecular level, one from the other.

Holy love is a love that makes distinctions. This is why the "love chapter" of 1 Corinthians 13 (which we should really read through a million times in a row if we're ever to truly understand what love is) notes that love "rejoices" with the truth. Real, unreasonable, overwhelming holy love is a love that says, "I love you so much that I will not stand by and watch you do this thing that will destroy you." Holy love discerns between what is good and what is not. True holy love places us in a special relationship that makes us the beloved object of God's holy love and guides and defines all of our other relationships.

Holy love makes distinctions between what is right and wrong. It takes account of what is really best for us. Sure, there may be rules, but they are not restrictive prohibitions so much as they are relational guidelines that ensure our ultimate freedom. Marriage, for instance, comes with a similar set of rules. If you think that you can get married and then sleep around with other people, you're not really looking for that special covenant love. Because you love your spouse, you willingly follow a set of guidelines that protect and nurture your love for one another. As you allow it to bloom, this love that is protected by healthy relational guidelines will bloom into something greater than you could have ever imagined in your wildest dreams.

Or, let's take an example from the world of sportsball. Let's say that you join the basketball team and your coach tells you that in order to play to the pinnacle of your ability, you will need to watch what you eat and cut out all soda. Because you are setting yourself apart (holiness) to do something that you love (basketball), you realize that soda and ice cream, as amazing as those things are, will not help you grow closer to what you love. In fact, the more you "cheat" on your diet, the less enjoyment you will get out of your devotion to being great at basketball.

In reality, Christianity has **never** been about a set of rules. As Dr. Cliff Sanders notes, "Holiness cannot be reduced to a series of behaviors; holiness cannot be reduced to a matter of outward conformity. Holiness must be a loving response to a personal God. And no one can love God or respond to God in love until one is fully and truly convinced that God loves him or her[37]."

If life with God isn't about conforming to a list of rules, then what is this Christianity thing really all about?

Who Is This God Person, *Anyway*?

God is holy love. There is nothing holy and there is not one drop of love apart from Him. He is the source of both. As Sanders further notes, "Holiness is never a fearful response to some wrathful deity who is simply in control of the world so that His subjects submit... holiness is a loving response - obedience and faithfulness - to a God who has loved us first[38]."

When we truly fall in love with God, our relationship with Him defines everything else for us. It is our love *for* Him that causes us to set ourselves apart from anything that would lessen that love relationship *with* Him. God is overwhelmingly loving, overwhelmingly forgiving, and overwhelmingly generous. Even when we falter, He is there to pick us up. Thus, life does not become about a list of rules that bind, but a pathway to becoming more like our beloved every single day. In this, we strive to take on the character of our beloved. When we become more and increasingly more like the character of God, we paradoxically become both more like Him and more fully ourselves.

Sanders notes, "What is fascinating to me is that when I began to understand holiness as love, I did find that I was separating myself from things that my church told me were bad. The difference is that I separated myself from these things because of my affection and desire to be separated *to* God, to be in a love relationship with God. The key here is we must understand the matter of a loving God as the root of all holiness[39]."

This truth should radically and forever reshape how we live. We cannot any longer play into the trap of the intergalactic seesaw. Neither the "holy roller" nor the "everything is love" attitude is fully a reflection of God's nature as holy love, so they must be rejected. We, as those following

Jesus, must be full of grace **and** truth if we are to become more like Him every day.

As Pastor Jimmy Evans has noted, "truth without grace is like surgery without anesthesia. Grace without truth is a pill bottle without any medicine40." It is only when we take on the fullness of both that we become like Jesus. Jesus is our example. He is what we must center our lives upon. We should no longer find ourselves attempting to discern which side of the seesaw is the correct one at the moment. The answer is always to examine the character of Jesus and uncover how holy love should guide our lives and each moment therein.

A Final Note on Holy Love As The Character of Jesus

If you cannot yet tell, I have a visceral reaction against the mottos of our day as it comes to love. Neither "love is love" nor "everything is love" are true as we define them. Knowing that there is **absolutely positively no such thing as love apart from the character of Jesus**, how can we then discover what love is?

The answer, of course, is simply to study the life and character of Jesus. There are at least two great lists in Scripture that explain or expound upon the character of Jesus, encouraging us to become more like Him every day. The first, not ironically at all, is the "love chapter" of 1 Corinthians 13. This is what you often hear at weddings, though it is woefully short when it is limited to human love interactions. It certainly includes that, but when you understand that 1 John 4:8 means that all love is really borrowed from the character of God, then you can read this list very differently, indeed.

First of all, you can (and should) re-read this list and replace the word "love" with the word "God." God is patient. God is kind. God is long-suffering. God keeps no record of wrongs. God does not rejoice in unrighteousness, but rejoices with the truth. And so on. When you replace "love" with God, you see how God truly loves you. This is not the end of the exercise, however.

Because we are to "be holy as God is holy," and our calling is to become more like Jesus today than we were yesterday, we can and should replace the word "love" with our own names. Lee is patient. Lee is kind. Lee always forgives… and so on. If what we call love flows from us differently than 1 Corinthians 13 describes, we have released something other than love.

For example, since love does not rejoice with unrighteousness, we cannot say that we are loving someone else if we excuse what God calls sin. However, in that paradoxical tension of holy love, neither can we say we are loving them if we hold their sin forever against them and refuse to help them seek God's best.

The other list is found in Galatians chapter 5. This is commonly called the "Fruit of the Spirit." While the Fruit of the Spirit listed in Galatians 5 begins with "love," what follows may be an explanation of what this love looks like. To take on the character of Jesus, which is the fullness of holy love, and discover the *freedom* (see the start of Galatians 5) that God offers through His love, these two sections of Scripture represent a good place to start.

> "But the fruit of the Spirit is love, joy, peace, patience, kindness, goodness, faithfulness, gentleness, and self-control. The law is not against such things. Now those who belong to Christ Jesus have crucified the flesh with its passions and desires. If we live by the Spirit, let us also keep in step with the Spirit. Let us not be conceited, provoking one another, envying one another" (Galatians 5:22-26).

One Final Ax Blow To The Intergalactic Seesaw

Perhaps the best illustration I have ever seen of this concept was given by my friend Joy Sherman. While preaching as the interim pastor at Meadow Park Church in Columbus, Ohio, Joy gave a message entitled "Half Full." The point of the message was that God is neither half true or half grace, but is fully both. While "truth" and "grace" are not rigidly synonyms for "holiness" and "love," there is a large margin of overlap.

Joy began the sermon with a physical seesaw already visible on the stage. As she explained the fullness of God, she held the seesaw so that one side was up and one side was down. She explained, as I have attempted to do in this chapter, how followers of Jesus often sit on one side or the other. Later, she held the seesaw directly in the middle, attempting to balance it on her hand, in order to show how we often try to make God half truth or half grace.

However, as she deftly pointed out, God is not half full. It was at this point that Joy went in an unexpected and different way. Utilizing an unseen hinge that was built into the plank of wood, Joy folded the seesaw upward and placed it back upon its base. The image was immediately striking. Here sat a seesaw with both sides at full mast. From a distance it looked very much like the shape of an upper case V.

It was here that Joy made her strongest point. God is not half grace. God is not half truth. God is paradoxically fully both. God is not half loving. God is not half holy and true. God is 100% holy love and neither love or holiness comes anywhere close to being real and true unless there is an absolute fullness to both.

I don't know about you, but I say it is time we take an ax to the intergalactic seesaw.

It was never all that fun in the first place.

[For Personal Growth]

Spend some time this week working through 1 Corinthians 13 and Galatians 5:22-26. Challenge yourself each day to compare one or more aspects of these lists with your own walk in life.

What is your next step towards becoming more like Christ?

[With A Group]

Go around the group and share where you, your family, the world your knew growing up, or current society sits on the intergalactic seesaw?

As a group, read and discuss 1 Corinthians chapter 13.

What surprises you? What challenges you? What are you noticing for the first time? What stands out to you?

Replace the world "love" with "God" and re-read the chapter out loud. How does this challenge you?

Replace the word "love" with your own name and reread the chapter, perhaps breaking off into pairs for the sake of time. How does this challenge you?

If there is time, share and discuss anything else from this chapter that challenged you.

Before you close in prayer, have each person share with the group what measurable and practical way you are going to respond to God this week.

[My Next Step]

[SIXTEEN]

GOD vs RELIGION'S UNHOLY ACCOUNTING DEPARTMENT

… With Liberty and Justice For All.

> "It is significant that Jesus attracted sinners
> while the Pharisees repelled them."
> **Warren Wiersbe, *Be Courageous, p 31***

God has brought the church I lead to some interesting places in our sermon series this year. A few months ago, we were in a series entitled *Religion Ruins Everything*. Throughout this series, we sought to give our people a new working definition of religion. "Religion is doing God's things, my way. It is trying to follow God without seeking the heart of Jesus." During this series, we took a hard look at how Jesus and religion were often at odds.

While I had known for decades that it was religion that killed the Lord Jesus, it wasn't until God led me to study more carefully Jesus' interactions with the religious leaders of His day that I realized just how at odds Jesus and religion really are.

I started to notice more and more carefully how everyone who was around the historical Jesus seemed to get better and draw closer to

God... except the religious. In fact, Jesus saved some of His harshest words for the religious leaders of His day. Between Jesus and His earthly cousin, John the Baptist, these religious leaders were often referred to as snakes and vipers who were really white-washed tombs. That may not sound like too harsh of a slam in today's vernacular, but, rest assured, these were beyond fighting words. These were some seriously harsh words coming from our Lord and Savior's mouth. This doesn't even get to the time He derided the religious Pharisees for trying to make converts, only to make them "twice the sons of hell you are." Dang!

Why would Jesus use such vitriol against the religious? After all, the scribes and Pharisees were never supposed to be the primary earthly antagonist in the Gospel narratives. In reality, the scribes and Pharisees were meant to be the Messiah's welcoming party. Their basic job description was to prepare the hearts of the masses to be ready for Jesus' coming into the world. So, what went wrong? Well, it is a long story, but to summarize; they fell more in love with rules than they did with Jesus.

Perhaps you haven't spent too much time studying 1st Century Middle-Eastern culture and history. No worries. Allow me to explain. No, there is too much. Let me sum up. In the Old Testament book known as the Exodus, a Jewish leader named Moses goes up a mountain and has an encounter with God. When Moses came back down to his people, he carried with him two tablets that contained God's Word for the Israelite people.

We often call the contents of these two tablets "The Ten Commandments," however, that was not their historical name. To our Jewish ancestors, they were called "The Decalogue," which means "Ten Words." These 10 Commandments, or Ten Words, became the backbone of a covenant God made with mankind. This "big 10" became the foundation for the law, which was completed (a little oversimplification for the sake of space) by the remainder of what we now call the Old Testament.

About a week ago I got a message from the man who served as my youth pastor when I was growing up. This was the man who presented Jesus to me in such a way that I decided to follow Him forever. This was the man who gave the chance for people who felt they were being called into a lifetime of ministry to respond and be prayed over. It was under Joe's ministry that I accepted Jesus, accepted a call to sexual purity, accepted a calling to ministry, preached my first sermon, led my first youth events, and completed my first internship on my way to a lifetime of vocational ministry.

Without Joe, I'm not sure where my life would be. I would not have gone to Oklahoma City to study for a life in ministry. I would not have met my wife. I would not have seen my son Logan come into the world. Renae and I would not have adopted our daughter Jazzy. I would not have spent six years in youth ministry, where my first funeral would be that of a young man who made a fatal decision when his girlfriend broke up with him. I would not have spent a season in Columbus, Ohio as Discipleship Pastor... and I certainly would not be serving as Lead Pastor of a church today. Joe's ministry had a sweeping impact on my life that I am forever grateful for.

Joe's message to me was a bold one. He began by noting that he had heard I was leading the church I serve through a ten week series on the Ten Commandments entitled #LifeIn10Words.

"I noticed you said you were preaching a series on the 10 Commandments. I'm sure I probably taught something like that before, too. However, and here's where the tricky part comes in... I don't believe the 10 Commandments are applicable to Christians today. Wow, that might be a bombshell..."

Perhaps if this e-mail had come to me just a few years earlier in my ministry, I would have been aghast. The 10 Commandments not applicable? How could a pastor say that? However, this word of cautious bomb-shellery had hit my inbox a few years after God had already been taking me on a journey through my own religious confusion.

Before we talk about that, let's look back at Moses and the story that leads to religious people killing Jesus. Moses comes down the mountain. The Israelites have already set up a Golden Calf that they are worshipping. Moses is angry. Things get broken. Israel pays the price for their sin. People agree that it is best to worship the One True God and things move forward.

Over the many years that follow the people of God have a habit of moving through seasons of intense devotion to God and seasons where they all but leave God behind. Perhaps it was this foolish cycle of seasons that causes some hyper-religious non-pan-dimensional beings to start tightening up their belts, so to speak.

Fast Forward to A.D. 30 (or so) and the people of Israel have been hoping against hope for hundreds and even thousands of years to see this Savior they refer to as the Messiah. This is the person, sent from God, who will be the culmination of everyone's hopes and dreams. There is just a little problem. The Messiah has been so long-awaited by this point and religious scholars have been given so much influence that they have created this oppressive system known as religion.

In this system, not only are people bound by the Big 10 (the Ten Commandments), as well as the entire law and prophets of the Old Testament, but by a total of 613 laws. These laws were passed down as tradition from generation to generation and there are supremely strict consequences for breaking these religious traditions in any way, shape, or form. While these rules, laws, and traditions were meant to guide the people of God, they became malformed, like our discussion of conscience in a prior chapter, and no longer honored God or caused people to seek after His heart.

Enter Jesus. Jesus, whom history and faith have proven IS the long-awaited Messiah these religious zealots were waiting for, immediately begins butting heads with the very people intended to be His welcoming party. Jesus had this annoying habit of taking the Old Testament laws and rules and redefining them. It wasn't that Jesus was changing them, as even He notes that He didn't come to abolish the law in any way, it was that He was fulfilling them and restoring their original heart-intention back to the forefront of conversation.

Let's take a quick look at just one of those conversations.

"Then Jesus was approached by Pharisees and scribes from Jerusalem, who asked, 'Why do Your disciples break the tradition of the elders? For they don't wash their hands when they eat" (Matthew 15:1-2 CSB).

Notice what these religious leaders bring to Jesus in the form of a complaint (a nasty habit religious people throughout history have had ever since). Jesus' followers were breaking "the tradition of the elders." In other words, they weren't following the rules that religion had created around the Law of God.

> "He answered them, 'Why do you break God's commandment because of your tradition?' For God said, 'Honor your father and mother; and, whoever speaks evil of father or mother must be put to death.' But you say, 'Whatever benefit you might have received

from me is a gift committed to the temple,' he does not have to honor his father.' In this way, you have nullified the word of God because of your tradition" (Matthew 15:3-6 CSB).

Did you catch that shade Jesus was throwing? These complaining religious leaders are whining to Jesus that His disciples aren't paying attention to the little rules they have put in place, while Jesus turns the tables on them and asks why they break God's heart-filled Law for the sake of their man-made traditions. Ouch.

Jesus quickly gets to the heart of the matter. He points out that while His disciples may have been breaking religious traditions, it was these religious leaders who were guilty. These shady characters had attempted to use the healthy practice of giving back to God from what He gives to us in order to get out of taking care of their parents.

They literally said, "oh, sorry mom and dad, but my money has to go to the temple, so I can't take care of your physical needs. Good luck with that." In the name of "devotion to God," they had attempted to cheat their own parents. Jesus would have none of it.

For Jesus, it wasn't about rules and traditions, it was about the condition of the heart. While I may be stepping on something I hope to write in a future book based upon the *Religion Ruins Everything* series we did at Sloan's Lake Church - itself loosely inspired by the series *Religious People Ruin Everything* by Faith Promise Church in Knoxville - I want you to notice what happens in Scripture when sinners get near Jesus... they get BETTER. Yet, look at what happens when the religious get near Jesus... they get BITTER.

Religion is all about putting people into boxes. Jesus' life-giving Gospel is about teaching people to love from a God-honoring heart. Religion is incapable of reaching the heart, so it produces all of the laws and rules it can to bind people into the path it wants them to walk.

Jesus came to set the captives free.

What does this have to do with my youth pastor and whether or not the Ten Commandments are still binding to those who follow Jesus?

You see, it all comes back to the heart. The problem for the pharisees was and still continues to be for religious people today that we are often more concerned with correcting people to adopt our religious traditions than we are with connecting people to the heart of Jesus so His heart can invade and reshape theirs.

Jesus connects us with the heart of God. When we connect with the Eternal, life-giving Spirit of God, we find something greater than rules and even greater than the Law, itself. In fact, as Scripture tells us, the Law (the Ten Commandments, as well as the Old Testament Law and Prophets) was only ever meant to lead us like a hand-maiden to Jesus Himself. When we connect with Jesus, we find something greater than the Law, we discover the heart of God and His expressed character.

Jesus spent a large portion of His ministry redefining for people what God had always meant in His law. He corrected our wrong thinking and expanded our view on so much of "the Law and the Prophets." Then, He fulfilled them. In that very moment when Christ's life was given on the cross, our need for the law was brought to its conclusion. Grace was now the leading force in our lives from that point forward. The Law was never the end God had in mind.

The apostle Paul, a follower of Jesus who just so happened to be a devout pharisee himself, spends a good deal of his own writings dealing with this topic of being free from sin and the even the letter of the Law. He tells the followers of Jesus who are wrestling with grace for the first time that we are now to be guided by the Spirit Himself. He tells us that the law was just a nurse who was supposed to take our hand and guide us to Jesus.

Yet, he still talks about this thing called sin. He tells his readers that there is still a set of choices that we can make that separate us from God. He asks whether the Christian should sin so that grace can increase. His answer is an emphatic "no!"

What my youth pastor was telling me, which I had been processing for a few years, myself, was that the Law no longer binds the Christian. The Law is no longer what is meant to guide us. The Law was only ever meant to show us just how incapable we are of saving ourselves. The Law was meant to point us to the only true source of life.

Joe, my former youth pastor, didn't mean that the Ten Commandments have no value at all. After all, we are NOT free to murder, commit adultery, slander one another, and dishonor our parents. Such things would be completely counter to the character of Jesus, and would be sin.

A walk of faith (which can include religion, but is not limited by its chains) is **not** about the rules. It is about walking with the Spirit of God and allowing Him to guide us. How can we possibly follow Jesus without any rules? How can there still be sin that breaks God's heart if the rules no longer apply? If we can't put God in a box and narrow Him down to a simple "do this, don't do that" list... how do we even follow Him?

What I'm about to share may be the most revolutionary thing I have ever come to study in God's Word. If not, it is really close. You see, religion misses the heart of God. The Bible, on every page, is constantly revealing to us the character of God. Jesus, God in earthly form, was the exact representation of the character of God. Jesus reveals God to us.

In his letter to the Galatians, the aforementioned Pharisee once known as Saul, writes a treatise on how our relationship to the Law has changed under the redemption of grace.

> "For the **whole law is fulfilled** in one statement; Love your neighbor as yourself. But if you bite and devour one another, watch out, or you will be consumed by one another. I say then, walk by the Spirit and you will certainly not carry out the desire of the flesh. For the flesh desires what is against the Spirit; these are opposed to each other, so that you don't do what you want. **But if you are led by the Spirit, you are not under the law**" (Galatians 5:14-18 CSB, Emphasis added).

What is this Pharisee turned Jesus-devotee saying? If we "walk with the Spirit" the law is not "over" us. That is a stick of dynamite in the closed fist of religion! Paul is saying that religion missed the mark. It was supposed to be about the heart of God, but was reduced to a list of rules.

Ironically, Paul goes on in Galatians 5:19-21 to list a bunch of stuff that the law spoke out against. He notes things like sexual immorality, idolatry, and the practice of banding together against a common enemy to destroy them (factions) as being against the heart of God. So, if Paul is so quick to list things that don't fit with God's heart, what is the difference between that and a list of rules?

What Jesus was saying all along was that it's not about lifeless rules, but about the life-giving Spirit of God developing His *character* in each of His followers. If you are constantly becoming more like the character of God, you don't need rules telling you what to do. You don't have to ask yourself, "should I cheat on my wife?," if you are becoming more like the embodiment of love, patience, and faithfulness.

You shouldn't have to ask yourself, "should I punch this guy out?," if you're becoming more like the embodiment of peace. Taking on the character of Jesus from deep within your transforming heart frees you from the rules. That doesn't mean you are free to go and break God's laws without consequence, it means you won't even desire to in the first place.

Sin is real. Sin breaks our relationship with Jesus and it breaks God's heart. The Law tried to litigate sin out of our lives, but that does nothing to remove the desire that lurks in our hearts. However, when we are falling in love with Jesus more and more each day, we no longer even WANT to do the things that break His heart.

When rules are in place, but our hearts desire that which the rules speak against, we do everything we can to find a way around the rules. However, when your heart is free from the bondage of the Law by grace, you simply no longer even desire to do those things anymore. Grace has the power to do what the Law never could, it transforms the very desires of the heart.

"But the fruit of the Spirit is love, joy, peace, patience, kindness, goodness, faithfulness, gentleness, and self-control. **The law is not against such things**. Now those who belong to Christ Jesus have crucified the flesh with its passions and desires. If we live by the Spirit, let us also keep in step with the Spirit" (Galatians 5:22-25 CSB, emphasis added).

While we should stand against sin, the strongest way we do that is to become more and more like God's perfect character. If we grow in self-control, we overcome sexual immorality. If we grow in faithfulness, we overcome idolatry. If we grow in kindness, we overcome hatred. If we grow in love and joy, we overcome selfish ambition.

The fruit of the Spirit is the character we begin to take on as we become more like Jesus every day. Unfortunately, even those who have been in church for much of their lives have been trained more by religion than by a relationship with Jesus. As soon as they accept Jesus in their lives, restrictive rules often come screaming back to the surface as the "pathway to holiness." We are so unaccustomed to being free, that the chains of religion seem inviting to us. So, we turn back to the rules, once again hoping that they will save us. They won't. It has never been about the rules.

From the beginning of time, it has always been about our holy communion with God through His Spirit. So, let's not complicate things more than we should. Take a breath. Close your eyes for a moment. Let your conscious mind feel the weight of the breath that flows in and out of your lungs.

The rules don't save you. Only Jesus' grace through faith does that. So, we must do as Galatians challenges us and walk with the Spirit each and every day. When we walk with the Spirit, the law - even then 10 Commandments - no longer serve us as our master, and we are free to take on the character of God.

So, how do you get to know Jesus better? How do you hear His heart? How do you come to take on the character that does not break, but fulfills the law and breaks the grip of sin?

The single most powerful thing you can do in your life is to set aside a little time each day to read your Bible and pray. While there are any number of spiritual practices this world will point you to in the name of "discovering your inner spirituality," there is nothing that compares to spending time in God's Word.

The Bible is God's love letter to you. It is living and active. Through God's Word, you discover the heart of Jesus. You see God's plans for your life. You uncover the fruit of Jesus' character and how it changed the world.

Spending a little time in God's Word each and every day is the single best and most definitive way of connecting with our utterly unreasonable God.

[For Personal Growth]

Have you placed your hope and trust in the rules, or do you live by the freedom of grace to become more like Jesus every day?

What in your life shows this to be true?

Spend some time this week reading and rereading Galatians chapter 5.

Each day, slow down a little more and listen a little longer for what God is saying to you.

By the end of the week, write down what you feel God is saying to you through His Word and decide on a (or some) measurable and practical steps that you will take to make this more a part of your life.

[With A Group]

Continue reading the next chapter before discussing both chapters as a group.

[My Next Step]

[SEVENTEEN]

CONFRONTING THE UNREASONABLE GOD
AKA The Un-finish-able Chapter.

> "... the Christ of the Gospel might actually seem more
> strange and terrible of the Christ of the church."
> **G. K. Chesterton, *The Everlasting Man,* p 193**

We have come a long way in this work towards better understanding the God who defined Himself by citing reality; "I AM that I AM." However, as explained in the opening paragraphs of this work, one could never exhaust the depths of who God Is. These few chapters have been but a skimming of the very first layer of atoms on the surface of all that is... Existence.

There is an infinite amount about God that I have no ability whatsoever to express in words, feelings, emotions, prayers, actions, or otherwise. God is. God IS. Would that we could leave it at that and fully understand the secret to life, the universe, and everything. God... Is.

We have come as far as I can currently take us on this journey. There are a great many other writers, pastors, and theologians who have written about God's nature and character. I suggest picking up one of their works and joyfully going onward. That being said, I wanted to let you in on a very unfinished understanding of what God has been showing me over the last few years.

God is completely and overwhelmingly unreasonable.

As I look back over my life, I realize that I do not deserve the blessings God has given me. From the family I was born into, to the opportunities that arose, and even in the prayers that went unanswered and the doors that slammed shut, God has always and in every way done above and beyond all that I could have imagined.

I'll be honest, there are times, perhaps more often than I care to admit, that I simply fail to see how this is the case. I look at what I don't have. I look at what I am up against. I look at the battle scars, and I don't see the blessing. Yet, in my more lucid moments, I realize that everything has worked together for my good. God has blessed me far beyond what my sinful heart has deserved in every whisper and every life-changing moment. I would wager that, should you listen carefully enough, this describes your life, as well. While I could point to almost any moment in my life and see the hand of God working in unreasonable ways for my betterment, the most recent season of my life stands out.

In 2016, I was an Executive Pastor of Discipleship for a larger multi-site church in Columbus, Ohio. Things were going great and plans were in place for me to become our next campus pastor as we looked to expand to a third location. As this was also the church's 50th Anniversary year, I had been working with our Senior Pastor on an expansive discipleship study that included highlights from our history, small group material, and a series of devotionals created by members of our congregation.

In the midst of preparing the 50th Anniversary material, Pastor Paul walked into my office and uncharacteristically stumbled over his words a bit. In short, he let me know that I needed to remove all references to him from the upcoming publication. While we had partnered together on this upcoming material in a wonderfully dynamic way, Paul had provided the framework, much of the content, and each of the sections had a word of wisdom directly from him.

I immediately knew that something was up, but waited for him to fill me in. Paul began to leave my office, paced outside of it for a moment, and then came back in, closing the door behind him. He then let me know that through a long season of prayer, his near future would likely see him becoming the Lead Pastor of another congregation.

Paul talked me through this transition and how he had wrestled with God for quite some time before arriving at the place where he would even have a conversation with another church. As far as Paul was concerned, he had felt he would spend the rest of his ministry serving right where he was.

This unexpected turn of events did, indeed, see Paul following God's calling to a new church just prior to the 50th Anniversary celebration. Because Paul and I had worked so closely together on this upcoming series, I was given the honor of walking both campuses of our church through our jubilee. Just knowing the powerful men and women who had proclaimed God's Word from that stage was humbling, and I was honored to be in that place for that momentous season.

Unbeknownst to me at the time, however, this also stirred something in me. I had long known that my calling was to ultimately step into a Lead Pastor position. In fact, prior to signing on with Pastor Paul, I was in serious talks with a church in Illinois to become their pastor. However, Paul's exceptional leadership and our strong synchronicity in ministry saw me joining his team... perhaps with a thought that I might one day follow him as pastor upon his retirement.

Something was rekindled in me as I lead our church through that momentous anniversary and got back into the pulpit each weekend. Though I did not actively seek to leave my then-current position, in the season that would immediately follow I began getting unsolicited phone calls from other churches. By the time I was talking with my third, fourth, or fifth church about becoming their pastor, I had to admit that God was up to something.

In the coming months I would find myself in serious consideration with four different churches across the country. This exciting season allowed me to prepare for some pretty bold moves. I am already a pretty straightforward person, however knowing that I didn't "need" to leave where I was at, and knowing that I continued to get calls from churches with an opportunity to pastor, I decided I would be as open and forward as possible with what I felt God was doing.

Over the years, I had become increasingly convinced that church could no longer be done the way it had been in the 1950's, 1990's, or even just five years prior and hope to reach the people God misses most and the next generation. At the time, I was reading books like Lee Kricher's amazing *For a New Generation* and devouring everything that Carey Nieuwhof was writing and podcasting. Everywhere I turned I saw the signs that revealed to me that church had changed more in the last 15 years than in the previous 150 combined.

I knew that, because of this passion in me to see things become different and more focused on reaching the people God misses most and helping people live Jesus-Centered lives, that I would not be a fit in many churches. I had seen too many of my friends step into a Senior/Lead Pastor position in an established church and begin to make changes, only to be asked to leave unceremoniously not that long after.

With each conversation I was having, I began leaning into the search teams more and more about the types of changes I was likely to bring. I plainly and openly told each church that if this was not what they were looking for, then let's end things right then and walk away as friends. I had no interest in seeing my head roll or the church blow up. Neither was appealing to me.

In the flow of these few months, I ended up narrowing the conversations down to two churches. One was in Ohio. One was in Denver. Having grown up in the Rocky Mountains, Denver was heavy on my heart. In fact, my wife had told me she felt God saying we were going to Colorado.

As things would have it, however, I got a call from the church in Denver letting me know that they were going with the other guy who was in consideration. Our interim pastor, Joy, and her husband, Steve, just happened to be with us in that moment. As I began to process what was happening, they told me "I feel like God is not done with this, yet."

Still, I didn't understand what was happening. I had really felt God moving in my heart towards the Rockies. My wife, who had told me prior to our move to Ohio that "I just feel like God is saying that the role He has for you doesn't even exist, yet." I didn't know how to process that, but in one of my early calls with Pastor Paul, he literally uttered the words, "the bones of this role are built on an old position, but the position we're calling you to doesn't really exist yet." How could she have called that one? And, yet, it seemed like Denver was a dead end.

Not that many days later, I got another call from the church in Denver. The other guy had gotten a very affirming vote from the congregation, however, both he and the elders had started to feel like this might not be the best fit. They wanted to know if I was still interested. I told them I would pray about it. My wife simply smacked me playfully and said, "see, I told you that was what God was doing."

Just a few short months later and I was stepping foot in Denver as the new Lead Pastor of Sloan's Lake Church, just as it was getting ready to celebrate its 130th anniversary. The ministry that was now called Sloan's Lake Church had been started when Colorado itself was just 11 years old!

A pioneer by the name of James Pollock had sacrificially paid to have the founder of the Church of God Reformation Movement come to Denver to share the hope that can only be found in Jesus. Then, Pollock paid the equivalent of $2,000 each and every month to see the ministry flourish.

And, flourish it did. Over the next 131+ years, what is now called Sloan's Lake Church created an improbable legacy in our city and across the globe. We would prove that "Innovation is our Tradition" by helping to plant churches across the state and founding ministries such as *The Severe Weather Shelter*. Started at and by our church, the SWS would expand into a network of 40+ churches dedicated to keeping our homeless neighbors alive during times of life-threatening weather.

This improbable impact would cause Denver's Mayor, Wellington Webb, to forever delicate January 28, 1998 as "Sloan's Lake Community Church Day" in Denver's history books. But, this was just one aspect of our legacy. Sloan's Lake Church directly and indirectly had helped to start ministries like *Heart to Honduras*, which has since planted over seventy churches in Honduras, Guatemala, Costa Rica, and more. We played a key role in the life of E. Faith Stewart, who would go on later in life to co-found *The Shelter* in Cuttack, India, in 1914. The Shelter has been helping to deliver girls from out of the jaws of the sex trafficking industry for over 100 years.

However, our world began to shift in profound and unexpected ways around the same time as we were getting that historic award. The rate of change in every area of life exploded, having unforeseen impact on every local church. Technology, travel habits, morals, shifting sports and school schedules, the explosion of single-parent homes, and more combined to create a new reality where attending church on a regular basis was no longer a societal expectation or norm.

As a result of this, our church came dangerously close to becoming one of the statistical 150 or more churches that close their doors forever every Sunday. But, this improbable church would not go down without a fight. Seeing the need for what experts now call "dramatic church revitalization," our retiring pastor made a bold challenge for the church to undergo dramatic change and do anything it takes (short of sin) to reach the next generation.

Prior to leaving my previous church, one of my leaders came up to me and, as she was saying goodbye, reminded me in strong words that a wise leader doesn't change ANYTHING in their first year at a new church. However, the hiring agreement the Sloan's Lake's elders signed as I came spelled out the fact that I was called to bring sweeping and radical change.

In that first year alone, it is not over stating things to say that we changed everything we could. Though I didn't fire anyone, the plan was already in place for the church staff to change, the style of music changed, every fake plant was removed and donated, walls were painted, bylaws were revised, our mission and vision was altered... In fact, as I look back, there are very few things that did not change and quickly.

As I've stated, this is often a recipe for disaster. I have known too many good people who have had their ministry cut short because of moves like this. Yet, the congregation, on the whole, not only accepted but embraced these changes. It certainly helps that the children and grandchildren who had left the church years ago were now coming back, but that level of change shook even me a bit.

It didn't take long for me to see how unreasonably great God was in all of this. I know a good majority of pastors who follow a long-tenured leader who have nothing but problems. Instead, I felt nothing but support. In fact, not only was the pastor I followed there in support of me on the day I was "installed," but his predecessor was as well.

I can't say just how powerful it is to have three generations of pastors standing together, the elders supporting the younger. I could cry even now thinking about it. But, their support didn't stop there. Both Ed and Gordon actually preached very forward-directed sermons as we entered our 130th Anniversary series, fittingly titled, "The Road Ahead."

I literally could not pay for the gifts I was given in this season. My predecessor, Ed Nelson, was an amazing and wise leader. As he prepared the church for his retirement, he told them time and again that they needed to hire a pastor who was at least 30 years younger than he. He told them almost weekly how the church was going to need to change. He reminded them regularly that I would be "green" and might come with some crazy ideas, but to embrace what God would do through my ministry and support me.

After I came, whenever someone from the church would go to him with an issue, he would simply refer them back to me and say, "talk to your pastor." I could cry just thinking of how much that means to me. I literally, in every way, could not have paid for, manipulated to get, or wiggled my way into a better place of support.

As I write this, the church is facing a season of bold decisions and sacrifice. Our ministry has changed dramatically, yet we still have a ways to go. As a 131 year old church, we also have a 60+ year old building that is in need of dramatic repair and renovation. We are also in that "mucky middle" of our transition where we are no longer what we were, but we are also not yet what we're going to be. We are very much in progress.

In spite of this, our elders decided to set forth with a bold vision "to have a transformational impact on 1% of our city, 1 person at a time." That is the "what we're called to do" behind our "why" of helping people live Jesus-Centered lives. But, we knew that this would require us to raise the level of giving and the overall look of our facility, as well as our reach into the community. In other words, it would take even bolder and BIGGER changes, a big blessing, and some big money.

Just a week ago, as I write this, I announced to the congregation the amazing news that a group of larger churches in our movement who had set aside grants for church planting had taken a chance on a 130+ year old church that is seeking and seeing dramatic revitalization. We would be receiving a grant, but there was a catch. In order to receive the grant, we would have to match the funds (or more). As I stepped down from the stage, a man in the congregation pulled me aside.

"How much do we have to raise?"

"At least $40,000."

"Put me down for the first 10," he said. I couldn't believe my ears.

God is overwhelmingly unreasonable.

He is unreasonably forgiving to those who have so desperately betrayed Him. He is unreasonably loving towards those who have utterly turned away from Him. He is unreasonably generous towards those who deserve nothing less than annihilation and wrath. God is utterly, in every sense of the word, unreasonable. And, literally, thank God for that.

This is what I am in the process of discovering in this step of my spiritual journey. Surprisingly, this journey has brought me back to the 10 Commandments, or what our ancestors called "The Decalogue" or "Ten Words." When we hear about the Ten Commandments, we immediately think "thou shalt not...," but these Ten Words have an even greater purpose than restraining or limiting what we're allowed to do.

As Professor of Christian Ethics David W. Gill has stated,

> "The Ten Commandments are a tenfold account of the ways to love God with all our heart, soul, strength, and mind and the ways to love our neighbor. They are at the same time the ten ways God loves us... The Ten Commandments are also a charter for freedom. They are the ten words of the God who delivered a people out of slavery and wishes to keep them free[41]."

While restrictive religion has shaped us to know the Ten Words only in the ways that they prohibit us, in reality, these are ten words of love that lead to abundant life. They are powerful words that will aim our life's journey towards its proper destination and also give us the grace we need to enjoy the road ahead. These are ten ways that God shows His love to us, and that is *powerful* to dwell on. They are ten words that set us free and help us live a life that is defined by love and joy.

In the book of Exodus, which is the account of God delivering His people out of the oppressive rule of Egyptian masters, we find the following statement: "Then God spoke all these words: I am the Lord your God, who brought you out of the land of Egypt, out of the place of slavery" (Exodus 20:1-2 CSB). In grave error, we often examine the Ten Words outside of their given context. Prior to giving us a list of (what many see as) rules, God first reminds us of WHO HE IS. He reminds us of His character. He reminds us of His unreasonable love for His children.

The Ten Words begins with a reminder that this is the God who brought us out of slavery. God's FREEDOM precedes anything that follows it. The

Ten Words are not religious restrictions that bind us, they are words of life given by a God who desires the best for His people and does not want them to fall back into slavery!

If Gill is right, then what follows in Exodus 20 is not a list of rules and restrictions, but, first and foremost, an explanation of ten ways that we love God, love others, and shockingly, the ways that God loves us! Gill's concept of this being how God loves *us* that haunts me. While we must absolutely make God *the* defining priority of our lives, the shocking truth behind the Ten Words is revealed as we walk through each Commandment.

God makes *us* His priority. He died to give us freedom. He desires for us to have a better life as we take on His character. He rested from His work, not because He needed it, but to give us an example of rest. He has given us a family and friends that surround and guide us. He protects us, even in unseen spiritual battles. He models the fullness of 1 Corinthians 13 love. He is more generous than we could ever hope to imagine. He guides us into truth and only speaks what is right over us. Finally, as Zephaniah 3:17 emphasizes, He not only created us, He sings songs of gratitude over us!

That is utterly unreasonable. I am still in progress on this understanding. I haven't gotten it down just yet. I'm letting you in on the rough draft. And, while your story may be different and my story isn't all that exciting, it is in the stories of our lives that we begin to see the tapestry of unreasonable love, unreasonable forgiveness, and unreasonable generosity that God has been weaving through our story since before we were even born.

As you examine your life, undoubtedly even in the toughest of journeys, you will find God's unreasonableness shine through. You will discover His holy love. You will experience the joy and peace He allows us to experience even when it doesn't make sense in light of what is going on. Even if we have experienced what feels like the worst that life has to offer, God unreasonably sacrificed His only unique and begotten Son on our behalf. He gave the first and best He had to offer. God literally tithed Jesus back to us, so that we would not face an eternity apart from Him.

God paid the price for our rebellion unreasonably. He gave until it hurt far more than we could ever imagine. And, for what? To reclaim broken sinners who constantly turn our backs on Him and chase after gods made in our own image. How unreasonable.

I'm still uncomfortable with this language a bit... God being unreasonable and all. It could be too easily misquoted or mistaken to mean something other than what I am intending and saying. And yet, I have not yet found a better terminology to explain what I see undeniably in front of me.

We serve an unreasonable God. We receive our freedom from an unreasonable God. We receive life more abundant from an unreasonable God. Thank God for that. Without that unreasonable love, grace, joy, peace, forgiveness, generosity, blessing, and sacrifice... we would all be lost.

As I study more on this concept, I continue to see the proof of it all across the pages of Scripture and the lives of others. There are so many places I could point to in God's Word where this truth has been hiding in plain sight. However, I could think of no better way to end this chapter, and even this unfinished journey than with this:

> "What then are we to say about these things? If God is for us, who is against us? He did not even spare His own Son but offered Him up for us all. How will He not also with Him grant us everything? Who can bring an accusation against God's elect? God is the one who justifies. Who is the one who condemns? Christ Jesus is the One who died, but even more, has been raised; He also is at the right hand of God and intercedes for us. Who can separate us from the love of Christ? Can affliction or distress or persecution or famine or nakedness or danger or sword?
>
> As it is written: Because of You we are being put to death all day long, we are counted as sheep to be slaughtered. No, in all these things we are more than conquerers through Him who loved us. For I am persuaded that neither death, nor life, nor angels nor rulers, nor things present nor things to come, nor powers, nor height, nor depth, nor any other created thing will be able to separate us from the love of God that is in Christ Jesus our Lord."
>
> Romans 8:31-39 CSB

[For Personal Growth]

How have you experienced Jesus' unreasonable love in your life?

Read Romans 8:31-39 every day this week. Each day, focus on a different promise that you see in the text.

[With A Group]

Go around the group and share how you have experienced God's unreasonable love, grace, forgiveness, and/or blessing in your life.

As a group, read and discuss Romans 8:31-39.

What surprises you? What challenges you? What are you noticing for the first time? What stands out to you?

[The Circle (Final Group Activity)]

Set aside some extra time for this final group study.

Begin by giving each person a coin, ball, or other small trinket. Beginning with the appointed leader (or someone brave), this person should give their trinket to one other person in the circle. They are then to give that person an encouragement and a challenge based on your time growing together.

The other person is *only* allowed to say, "Thank you," and may put that trinket into a bowl or other designated container.

This person then gets the opportunity to give their trinket to someone else in the circle and do the same.

Continue as long as the Holy Spirit leads.

Bring tissues.

[EIGHTEEN]

THE SODA CAN FLOATING IN THE OCEAN
And Other Tales that Have No End

> "If there is a God, it should be your life's business to know
> Him correctly for Who He Is and what He respects."
> **Dr. Cliff Sanders**

It does not pain me in the slightest to say that this book is wholly incomplete. Truly, the subject matter itself could never be complete. Trying to say "this book contains everything there is to know about God," is like a soda can reveling in the fact that it has swallowed the ocean, when, in reality, it is only full of itself.

That soda can may be full, but the oceans rage on past the horizon. This is a little bit of what one faces when writing a finite book on the subject of the infinite. To say that this book is a complete account of God would be utterly laughable.

One of my favorite verses in all of Scripture has to be John 21:25.

"And there were also many other things that Jesus did, which, if every one of them were written down, I suppose not even the world itself could contain the books that would be written" (CSB).

This book has been a story about God, but it is also a story about you. It's not just the things written in the Bible that this verse speaks to, you see, it's what Jesus is doing in our lives and the lives of people all around us. Our lives are the stories that God is telling. If the tales of how God's story invaded and reshaped each of our own personal stories were written down, not a single library on earth could contain the books that would be written.

You have a story to tell. You may not think that it is a great story, but no one else in history can tell the tale that your story tells. Your story can make a difference. The life you have lived, the struggles you have faced, the things you have overcome, and the bonds you have made are more than just a story worth telling; they are a part of the story God is telling.

Your story may not seem like much to you, but it may just be the story God uses to change someone else's life. My hope in writing this book is that you would begin to examine God's story. I pray that you seek to become more like Him every day. The reality of God's grace, however, is that as you become more like Jesus, you also become more truly yourself.

It has been said that God has only one treasure in the universe, and that is human beings. I believe it. Your story isn't through yet. Every one of us has a story to tell. Every saint has a past. Every sinner has a future.

God is unreasonably in love with you. My hope is that this book will inspire you to learn more about God's story. As you do, I am certain that you will have a greater and greater story to tell about how God's story has invaded and reshaped your story.

Perhaps you've read this far and still don't believe that God exists. My greatest thought on this is that, for the sake of us all, please prove it. If God does not exist, we all need to know. If, however, you discover that God truly does exist, you'll have done something greater for yourself than you could have ever imagined.

After all, who we say God is is truly the deepest layer of our reality. It shapes and influences everything else that we say, think, or do. Perhaps you are trying to find answers in life. Perhaps you are still seeking the answer to life, the universe, and everything.

May I suggest that it would be better if you started with the question. **THE** question behind life, the universe, and everything.

Who Is This God Person, *Anyway*?

[*NOTES*]

1 J. B. Phillips, *Your God is Too Small* (New York: Touchtone Books, 1997), 9.

2 Craig Groeschel, Gen. Ed., *What is God Really Like?* (Grand Rapids: Zondervan, 2010), 142.

3 Ted Dekker, *The Slumber of Christianity: Awakening a Passion for Heaven on Earth,* (Nashville: Thomas Nelson, 2005), 199.

4 Craig Groeschel, Gen. Ed., *What is God Really Like?* (Grand Rapids: Zondervan, 2010), 113.

5 See https://careynieuwhof.com/episode171/

6 Lucas Miles. *Good God: The One We Want to Believe in But Are Afraid to Embrace,* (Franklin: Worthy Publishing, 2016), 16.

7 Ibid., 60-61.

8 Cliff Sanders, *Making Sense Out of Spirituality,* (Oklahoma City: MACU PRESS, 2008), 24.

9 Ibid., 31.

10 Brennan Manning, *Abba's Child: The Cry of the Heart for Intimate Belonging*, (Colorado Springs: NavPress, 1994), 62.

11 Ibid.

12 J. B. Phillips, *Your God is Too Small* (New York: Touchtone Books, 1997), 19.

13 James Bryan Smith, *The Good and Beautiful God,* (Downers Grove: InterVarsity Press, 2010), 59ff.

14 Ibid.

15 Kara Powell, Jake Mulder, and Brad Griffin, *Growing Young: 6 Essential Strategies to Help Young People Discover and Love Your Church,* (Grand Rapids: Baker Books, 2016), 144.

[16] Ibid., 157

[17] Ibid., 157

[18] John Ortberg, *Who Is This Man?,* (Grand Rapids: Zondervan, 2012), 12.

[19] Ibid., 15

[20] Channel Matthew Santoro, *10 Most Influential Books of All Time,* published March 20, 2018. https://www.youtube.com/watch?v=G7kow44p8vc. Accessed May 5, 2018.

[21] John Ortberg, *Who Is This Man?,* (Grand Rapids: Zondervan, 2012), 14.

[22] C. S. Lewis, *Mere Christianity,* (San Francisco: Harper Collins, 2001), 52.

[23] J. B. Phillips, *Your God is Too Small* (New York: Touchtone Books, 1997), 15.

[24] Ibid., 15ff.

[25] Ibid., 16.

[26] Ibid., 16.

[27] Francis Chan, *Forgotten God: Reversing Our Tragic Neglect of the Holy Spirit,* (Colorado Springs: David C. Cook, 2009), 46.

[28] Ibid., 70

[29] Matthew B. Sims, *A Household Gospel: Fulfilling The Great Commission in Our Homes*, (Simpsonville: Grace For Sinners Books, 2013), 14.

[30] Cliff Sanders, *Making Sense Out of Spirituality,* (Oklahoma City: MACU PRESS, 2008), 42.

[31] Warren W. Wiersbe, *Be Diligent: Serving Others as You Walk With the Master Servant,* (Colorado Springs: David C. Cook, 1987), Loc 5558.

[32] Reggie Joiner, Orange Conference, April 30-May 2, 2014

33 David Aukerman, et. al, *Holiness: A Lenten Devotional,* (Anderson: Church of God Reformation Movement, 2018), 5.

34 P. T. Forsyth, *The Work of Christ,* (Hempstead: Hackney College), 126-127.

35 Simon Ponsonby, *The Pursuit of the Holy: A Divine Invitation,* (Colorado Springs: David C. Cook, 2010), 29.

36 The Church Leaders Podcast, July 17, 2018 - Julie Slattery: Embracing a Biblical Narrative of Sexuality

37 Cliff Sanders, *The Optimism of Grace*, (Oklahoma City: MACU PRESS, 2017), 150.

38 Ibid.

39 Ibid.

40 Jimmy Evans, Gateway Conference, 2012

41 David W. Gill, *Doing Right: Practicing Ethical Principles,* (Downers Grove: InterVarsity Press, 2009), 327-330.